PRAISE FOR *RISK TAKER*

Brian Aspinall does it again. He offers relatable information to help learners navigate through the world of coding and beyond. Integrating technology through curriculum is the key to developing natural learning opportunities. He sees that it is not about the device or program, but rather what can be done with it that is empowering to students. His talent of connecting with students to help them become leaders of their learning is incredible to witness. Rather than giving a recipe to produce the same result, his guiding efforts give the tools that empower the learner to create their own path. Building relationships is the key foundation for learning and one which Brian both understands and represents in his books.

Laura Kennedy, Educator, Halifax, Nova Scotia

Brian continues to engage us all in meaningful and purposeful conversations around education, STEM and leadership. His passion and commitment to taking risks is contagious and evident in his energy and content that he represents.

Maggie Fay, Educator & Author of Hallway Connections

Leave it to Aspinall to raise and lift teacher voices from across the globe into one powerful edition. There is no better read for educators whether you are new or a veteran. You will be inspired!

Ms. Deb Hake, Educator, California, USA

PRAISE FOR *RISK TAKER*

Picking up where his past books (Code Breaker and Block Breaker) left off, Risk Taker offers hard truths and inspiration for teachers in an ever-changing educational landscape. Brian finds the same balance between personal stories and progressive pedagogy in this book that he has mastered in his high-energy presentations and workshops. Educators in any role will find uplifting reminders that we're all in this together, and that amazing things can happen when we're willing to take some risks.

Jeff Hennigar, Educator, Halifax, Nova Scotia

Brian Aspinall taps into the importance of engaging and empowering kids through the use of not only innovation, but more importantly, by connecting with and developing real and meaningful relationships with kids. His books give voice to educators who are excited about sharing ideas, and empowering students to think, learn, and create without conventional borders. Brian has encouraged and provided opportunities for both kids and educators alike to value the process over the product, to make mistakes, and to learn, explore and experiment fearlessly. Welcome to the culture of risk takers!

Christi Benoit, Educator, Winnipeg, Manitoba

PRAISE FOR *RISK TAKER*

Risk Taker is a fantastic piece of work. Not only does Brian take a risk with this, but he gives others the ability to showcase ways they have taken risks throughout their lives and careers. If you haven't read Brian's work, start with this book, then go to his "Code" series. You'll love this book as a way to improve yourself, not because you are an educator, lawyer, engineer, or student. This is a book that won't ever become dated!

Jeff Kubiak, Educator, Author of One Drop of Kindness

Brian is always sharing his stories of taking risks to disrupt the status quo in education, not just to make it different, but to make it better. Who better to write a great book to challenge us all to be risk takers and disrupters! Thank you Brian.

Chris Woods of dailySTEM, Educator, Presenter, Podcaster, Author

This isn't a book about why technology is important for our students. This is a book about changing the education game, about being better, about self-reflection, about learning and growth. Brian reminds us that it is in our mistakes where learning happens and it is in our self-reflection where change and growth begin. Risk Taker is authentic, genuine and honest. Risk Taker is the book about education we've been waiting for!

Daphne McMenemy, Educator, Author of Gracie

PRAISE FOR *RISK TAKER*

Being a risk taker isn't something that comes easy in today's society. Although it is my belief that we are all constantly taking risks on a daily basis even if we are not fully aware. I also believe it takes a unique kind of individual to inspire others to step out and try something new. Throughout Brian's multiple books he shares real life examples of the ways these risks are taken within the school community. Whether it is a teacher attempting coding with their students, or any other new idea that is outside their normal or it might be the teacher who is being openly transparent with their students inspiring them to take risks to improve themselves, Brain taps into his colleagues and shares their stories so that others may learn, grow and be encouraged to take their own risks. Through following Brian's journey, reading his multiple books and engaging in a variety of conversations I continue to learn so much. It is my hope that through reading stories and examples from all over, you are also inspired to try something new and become a more confident risk taker not just for your students but for you!

Nicole Kaufman, Educator Avon Maitland District School Board

01010010 01101001 01110011 01101011

RISK TAKER

Strengthen your courage, blaze a new trail and ignite your students' passions!

BRIAN ASPINALL

RISK TAKER

Copyright © by Brian Aspinall
First edition January, 2020

All rights reserved.

No part of this publication may be reproduced in any form, or by any means, electronic or mechanical, including photocopying, recording, or any information browsing, storage or retrieval system, without permission in writing from both authors.

www.mraspinall.com
www.brianaspinall.com

For those educators who have taken a risk on me.

I am forever grateful.

CONTENTS

GRIT

MODIFICATION

AUTHENTICITY

IMPACT

DETERMINATION

UNAFRAID

HONESTY

PERSEVERANCE

CHANGE

MINDSET

NETWORKING

TENACITY

COURAGE

RISK

FOREWARD

'Adam – forget the rules.'

As a young Assistant Principal, those three words were perpetually at the forefront of my brain as a 29-year-old newly minted leader setting up my office and meeting staff for the first time.

They weren't words I heard at some leadership conference or read in a book. They were self-imposed and became one of my leadership mantras.

I'm of course not advocating anything illegal – dangerous – or even something that may put your leadership position at risk.

Just forget the rules now and then.

I can vividly remember a conversation with one of my nine yard supervisors that helped to supervise the 1,200+ students at our Kindergarten through fifth-grade school each afternoon during lunchtime.

The logistics alone of feeding that many children within a ninety-minute time span can warrant enough colour-coded spreadsheets to stifle even the most organized person.

And let me tell you, that first day of school during lunch was bonkers.

There had been some semblance of organization and a plan from the previous leadership team, and without knowing specifics I'm sure it was successful. But what went down on my first day – as the 'leader of lunch' – did not go down in an organized way.

Every first grader was lost and asking for their teacher. The battery in my walkie-talkie went dead because I was brand new and didn't think about charging it the day before. When the first graders were leaving the cafeteria and second-grade was coming in, they did so through the same double doors.

At the same exact time.

Now try and picture me. Twenty-nine years old, brand new slacks, crisp white shirt neatly ironed, brand new tie, shined up brown leather shoes, my walkie-talkie is dead, I didn't yet have a whistle on my key ring and a few hundred seven- and eight-year-olds are completely scattered like a line of ants that just had their column disrupted. The louder I raised my voice to attempt any sort of organization, it seemed the hoard of hungry children would just increase their volume and disarray amongst themselves.

I made two decisions that day.

The first was to stop talking – stop directing – and let the crowd find where they needed to go.

Other than the new first-grade students, all the others had already been through the cafeteria in preceding years. My hope was that instinct and muscle memory would kick in and they would all find a place to sit and fill their tummies with whatever nourishment they had that day.

Sometimes you don't need to try and solve a problem. Sometimes all you need to do is be quiet, take a few steps back, and let things unfold how they'll unfold.

Once lunchtime was finally over (probably the longest ninety minutes of my life), I called an emergency meeting of the nine lunch supervisors we had that day. We'd only briefly met two hours earlier just before lunch kicked off and I didn't even know all of their names.

"What happened at lunch today?"

"It was complete pandemonium."

"We can't keep doing this for the next 179 days of the school year."

"Why does everyone enter and exit out of the same set of doors, at the same time?"

And then it happened. The 'lead' amongst the women raised her hand and offered a response.

"These are the rules, Mr. Adam. We've been doing this for the past three years, they're the rules. We're just following the rules."

It was then that I made my second decision for the day. I looked all nine of them in the eyes.

"We're going to forget the rules and create our own."

We then assigned different people to role play as if they were a child. Having one grade level enter through one set of doors that opened directly onto the path they used when coming from their classrooms. Change was starting to happen and it looked promising.

Looking around the cafeteria there were four sets of double doors. It seemed completely obvious to me – so I asked the question.

"Why don't we use a different set of doors to have kids exit through once they've been dismissed? It's on the opposite side of the entrance doors and it leads directly onto the playground."

Looks – whispers – and then someone spoke.

"We had that idea years ago but were told it wasn't part of the established rules."

Nothing needed to be said, this group of women who opened up yogurt containers on a daily basis – solved disputes on the playground – and knew a thing or two about kids, knew exactly what I was going to say.

"We can do whatever we want – and we're going to forget the old rules and make up our own."

And that's exactly what we did.

The next 179 days of lunch weren't always completely smooth, but each one was better than the last. And something else happened each day.

The nine fabulous ladies started solving other problems, both old and new.

Doesn't make sense to have every single student go back to class after they eat to drop off their lunchbox before playing.

Let's buy some cheap laundry baskets, have kids drop them in there, and have only two children go back to class each day to drop the entire basket off.

Having the teachers walk to the playground after lunch to pick up their classes was causing some problems. It takes up their lunchtime and also eats into instructional minutes.

We assigned student line leaders to walk the classes back. It gave kids leadership opportunities and built goodwill among the teachers.

Now before you get excited forgetting all the rules, this idea does not apply to every leadership decision or situation you're going to be involved with. It's important to be constantly weighing the risk of those decisions against any number of factors.

What's been done in the past?

It's always a smart decision to know the history of a rule before you go about trying to make a new one. Every problem has a solution and your 'new' solution may have already been tried. Don't give up on your idea, it may just need some tweaking or adjusting before it's completely dialed in.

Will you get in trouble? Or worse, lose your job.

There are potentially some serious ramifications when forgetting the rules – and it's imperative to complete those risk assessments against a more favorable outcome to your current situation.

Will anyone get hurt?

Are you breaking any laws?

Is this something you'd want spread across social media?

It's admirable to believe in change so much that you're willing to put yourself out there. Just stop and think about those risks. Sleep on your new idea. Talk with a few friends or colleagues who are confidential and can give you pragmatic input. And above all else, make sure that you can live with and stand behind your decision. You're an educator, you made a decision, and that means you have to stand behind what you did.

Pro Tip: If your organization or community isn't used to a 'forget the rules' kind of culture, start with small and lower impact decisions to warm them up. Choose your rules wisely and carefully – I'd rather have five small wins than one big disastrous failure and then you for sure won't be able to tackle any of those big ones – your trust will be gone.

Pain points are a great place to start:

- Organizational culture.
- What type of coffee is available to employees.

- Paperwork and the approval process for getting reimbursed.
- The flow of kids through the cafeteria during lunch.

Pain points that cause friction and productivity with your people and within your organization is a great place to start forgetting the rules. If you always follow all the rules, you're never going to solve real problems that weigh you and your organization down.

And dang it – if you always follow the rules, you're never going to reach your full potential or that of those that you lead. Don't let small mundane problems keep you from doing the real work that you're meant to be doing.

Don't think outside of the box – get rid of the box.

I don't want to be constrained by only being able to think inside or outside of the box. Break it down, put it in the recycle bin and do what you think is best for your organization. Take the risk!

Adam Welcome (@mradamwelcome), Educator, Speaker, Author, Runner

01010010 01101001 01110011 01101011

> *"I am free, no matter what rules surround me. If I find them tolerable, I tolerate them; if I find them too obnoxious, I break them. I am free because I know that I alone am morally responsible for everything I do."*

Robert A. Heinlein

#RiskTakerEdu

01010010 01101001 01110011 01101011

GRIT

Dear Students,

Your intelligence cannot be measured by a number. Your intelligence is defined by your willingness to learn and try new things. You are more than a number. You are a brilliant person with unique ideas. Share them!

Sincerely,
Your Teachers 🤍
#RiskTakerEdu

The Toronto Raptors won their first NBA title in June, 2019, backed by thirty-seven million Canadian fans from coast to coast. It is quite remarkable how sports can unify a nation and bring people together to celebrate tremendous success. There was a certain aura that day, something in the air that was giving us all a little extra zip in our step. For many, school was out for summer. For some, like us, we still had a few weeks to go. Many were putting the pen to paper and scribbling out their graduation speeches while watching the basketball game highlights on YouTube. What a time to be alive! I couldn't help but rewind the clips and listen to each player's response to the TV personality.

"What did it take to get you guys here?"
"Hard work."
"Determination."
"Grit."
"Rigor."
"Perseverance."
"Teamwork. We have a GREAT group of guys!"

Of course, talent was also involved. So was math. Plenty of math. Whether we look at the now historic buzzer beater shot made by Kawhi Leonard to advance Toronto to the Eastern Conference Finals or just explore game stats and data. This is what makes math beautiful. This is what makes learning beautiful.

> "Know the rules well, so you can break them effectively."
>
> - The Dalai Lama
> #RiskTakerEdu

Sometimes our best ideas come from unique experiences we never saw coming.

Leonard, the former new King of the North, wears a number two on his jersey. Number two. The only even prime number. The base of every computer system. The root of doubling. The main ingredient used in halving. The number two. This tidbit of information could easily form a full day of lesson activities.

"What is your favourite number? Why?"

Always ask why. Asking why is what this book is about. I've written about technology. I've written about coding. I've written about Minecraft. It has been a fantastic ride both personally and professionally and I am now eager to share some hard truths. Why? Because it is in the best interest of our students.

"Now that you have won an NBA championship, what will you do next?"

"Celebrate with my teammates!"

I love this response. They also mentioned living in the moment and dealing with other people later. If you have been following my blog, I have made it my mission to amplify teacher voice and lift others up. For some reason the second an educator decides to pursue a leadership role, they immediately become gossiped about in the staffroom. Gossip is toxic for any community. I've been gossiped about and even done it myself. I'm sure you have too. It is not a great feeling. If I can lift up two people each morning, I, in turn, lift myself up. When we help others, we help ourselves. When we gossip about others, we hurt ourselves. Celebrate with your teammates.

> *Students will strive to live up to what you believe of them. So think very highly of them.*
>
> *#RiskTakerEdu*

I wish I could gather a word art picture from all the graduation speeches given this year. I imagine it would mimic the words spoken by the Raptor's last night. Determination. Hard work. Perseverance. When I was still in the classroom, I remember suggesting that a simple way to improve math scores was to focus on organization, not more math. There is a misconception that *more* means better. This is definitely not the case, especially in mathematics, and *more* yields this notion that math is a score. I've written before that math is not a score, golf is. The problem with scoring anything at school is that we create a level of competition. Grades sort kids. Grades hurt kids. Grades harm kids. A bold claim, but I stand by it. As long as we have grades, we will have cheating. Kids only cheat to achieve a grade or a prize or bragging rights. School should be about learning. When I hear about students cheating on exams with cell phones, I immediately want to ditch the exams, not the phone.

Of course, knowledge construction is vital and I am not suggesting we use phones as a crutch. But I believe they have a place and can provide a massive level of equity for students who might require assistive technology or access in general.

Back to the Raptors. Imagine their training program. Imagine their practice drills. Think for a second how the environment becomes their third teacher. The size of the court. The height of the basket. The circumference of a basketball. The number of laps they run. The number of layups they make. Using that square on the backboard to help make two point shots. AH! The number two. It is beautiful, isn't it?

But I Don't Like School!
By Christi Benoît (@msbenoitsclass)

We have all known a student who claims to not like school. When asked why, that child may claim "because, I just don't like it" and leave it at that. When I first began teaching, it was like I was setting out on a mission. My goal was to seek out those *I don't like school* kids and turn them into educational enthusiasts! Simple, right?! Well, my eager, fresh-out-of-university self sure thought so!

I spent my first four years of teaching in the Nursery / Kindergarten world. My Nursery / Kindergartens *loved* school! Everything was new, play-based, and exciting! I could do almost anything and they would eat it right up! (Literally and figuratively: "Don't eat the Play-Doh: A Memoir" could easily be the title of my book if I ever write one!) However, two years ago I moved on up to the big leagues: *grade one*. It was here in this new classroom that was not filled with toys, a sandbox, or water table, that I had a *big* wake up call, and I realized I would have my work cut out for me.

The first week was great! We engaged in various activities that allowed us to build community, have fun, and get to know one another. However, once we settled into our routine and items like literacy and math groups were in full swing, I began to notice something. It was subtle at first, but as the days progressed, it became more and more obvious. And here it is, folks… in grade 1… some kids, dare I say it… DON'T. LIKE. SCHOOL. There, I said it. Before I venture off, let me add one very important detail. I have the honor of teaching in a school with inner city characteristics . I was raised by an amazing, hard working single mother of two in a low-income provincial housing complex. The community where I teach and learn is beautiful for all the diversity, stories and culture that it has to offer. However, like anything, it also has its challenges. Poverty is a common factor in our school community. Students often come to school with a great deal weighing on their minds. I make it my sole mission to meet their social emotional needs as best I can; as educators I think we can all agree that it is very difficult for a child to learn if that child has a sad heart, scary thoughts in their head, not enough food in their tummies, or is unsure as to where "home" might be next.

It can be difficult to juggle all the needs in the classroom, but we are teachers, and that is what we do. But this one little guy who sat in my classroom during our instructional learning time, with his hood pulled up over his head, was really adding a whole new element to my juggling act. No matter what I tried, no matter how "fun" or engaging I tried to make reading and writing, his response was simple.

"I DON'T LIKE SCHOOL!"

When I would try and pry a little further, he would usually respond with the following answer:

"It's too hard."

This sweet, young, impressionable boy in my classroom, at the young age of six years old, already believed that he wasn't "smart." It broke my heart and I tried everything to try and build up his confidence; I gave him leadership roles, I provided him with alternative seating, I even let him build a fort to do his work inside of! These attempts seem to be "band-aid fixes". But then something amazing happened. We did our first STEAM activity. This little guy who spent most of his days using every avoidance strategy in the book began to shine like never before.

Our STEAM challenge that day had students creating a wearable device using the provided materials that would protect one of the body parts associated with the five senses. At first I was nervous as this challenge could be tricky. I had visions of my little friend having a complete meltdown at the first inconvenience. This is one of the few times I can say, I was *happy* I was *wrong*. I stood back and watched my students excitedly get to work; I kept an extra eye and ear on my little friend. I watched as he held a piece of construction paper in his hand. He moved it close to his face and began to bend it gently across his eyes. I watched as he grabbed a pair of scissors, some tinfoil, and some tape. I had never seen him so focused! It soon became clear that this little guy was on his way to making some pretty stylish glasses! A few times he tried them on, and noticed they were a little too small.

Instead of giving up, he just got right back to work! Cutting, taping, adding tinfoil; it was amazing. By the time he was finished, he was so excited to show me his product he could hardly talk without tripping over his words! You know what he said next? Mark my words:

"Can I make something else?!"

I could hardly believe my ears! I told him he was an amazing engineer and that I couldn't *wait* to see what he created next! His face beamed with pride! Before the lunch bell rang, I took him by the hand down our hallway so he could show off his amazing creations to the other teachers and kids down our hallway. He couldn't *wait* to show his work and explained how he did it with pride. As we walked back to our classroom, that little guy looked up at me, and with a huge smile on his face, said "I actually am pretty smart" and let me hug him!

Not all kids come to school having had someone in their home tell them how smart, amazing, or wonderful they are. And that is not because of a lack of love; It's often just the product of circumstance. Although I told that little guy countless times a day how smart and amazing I believed he was, he needed opportunity to believe in himself. My words of encouragement were no longer empty ones, they carried truth. If there is one thing I hope my students learn during their time in our classroom, is that they are *all* learners. They *all* have the power to achieve great things. Most importantly, I hope that my students learn to believe in themselves. I know I believe in them.

01010010 01101001 01110011 01101011

MODIFICATION

Dear students:

We are not going to tell you about the jobs of tomorrow because you are the ones who will create them! Be bold, be creative and be YOU! But remember to also be kind. You can never lose if you are kind.

We believe in you.
Your Teachers 🤍
#RiskTakerEdu

Remember Columbia House? I used to join, quit, join, and quit again to try and get dozens of albums for only a penny. To think CDs are dated technology makes me feel old. But not having a penny being made in Canada any longer makes me feel ancient! Canadian youth of today will hear and read about CDs and pennies and think it was the dark ages. Imagine today being thought of as the dark ages?! In fact, to quote my good friend Sunil Singh (@Mathgarden), the rate of change today is the slowest it will ever be. This holds true tomorrow, next week, next year, and so on. And yet school is one of the slowest moving parts of this world. As a former principal once stated, if school was a business we would all be bankrupt because we are so slow to change.

Complacent is a word I recently heard used to describe staff members. This suggests staff are content where they are and happy with what they do. However, we never expect students to be complacent. We expect them to move. We expect them to grow. We got into this business as life-long learners so being complacent is not acceptable. It is OK to be where you are. It is not OK to stay there. The Latin root of complacent means "very pleased," and even though this staff was pleased with themselves, the administrator was not so pleased with them.

"This is a tough school," I was told. I've heard this countless times and each time, I shudder. Such a terrible label. Such a terrible way to view people. I don't think there are bad kids, just young kids who might make uninformed choices and need a little guidance. For many, school is the only safe place. When students show up late, greet them and thank them for coming to school rather than punish them for tardiness.

"This is a tough school."

> *Our worst day at school might still be better than one student's best day at home. Having some perspective helps develop positive rapport.*
>
> *#RiskTakerEdu*

Tough, by definition, means to be strong enough to withstand adverse conditions. Sounds like a compliment to me. However, when used in a school context, it typically means kids are not compliant. Ironically, program determines behaviour, so let us just see how "tough" kids are when we don't bore them with busy work. I would argue that "tough" students just need an opportunity to be innovative.

What secret talents do they have? Are we are of them? How can we unlock them?

Like most schools, there are pockets of innovation. I know those educators. They live and breathe school. You know them too. In fact, you are probably one of them. They are the ones closing the door to bend the rules slightly to engage their students further. They are the ones typically isolated and often gossiped about for being "different" in the way they instruct lessons. They are the ones usually talking less and listening more. They are the ones I want teaching my kids. You won't typically find them standing in line to use the photocopier.

But, without good leadership and innovative teaching methods, why would anyone seek out to change? Change sounds scary. However, in a world that changes overnight, the only strategy guaranteed to fail is not trying something new. It is OK to be where you are, but it is not OK to stay there.

When I am asked to define or describe the characteristics of being a good leader, I immediately think of Airbnb and Uber—two of the biggest companies in the world, yet they do not sell their own product or service. Leadership is not about demonstrating your power, but rather by showing how powerful your staff and students are. In fact, I could care less what your role is in school. Your action and example make you a leader. I'm very fortunate to visit schools across North America and I have come to notice the second I walk in the front door I can sense the community—good or bad. The schools where kids seemed most engaged have leaders who are in the trenches with them, not behind an office door. The rapport, high fives, and conversations about other things unrelated to school are what makes these schools unique and special.

When MakerEd & Community Connect
By Jeff Hennigar (@MrHennigar)

Recently I agreed to take part in a project that would become the most community-involved in-school project that I've been a part of. A colleague from Brilliant Labs, Sarah Ryan, suggested I work with her on a project in conjunction with the Neil Squire Society; an organization that works to empower people living with physical disabilities. Sarah proposed the idea of having my fifth-graders design and 3D print assistive devices. I did some digging and found out that 3D printed assistive devices are at least 90% more cost effective than buying them commercially. For someone living with a condition such as arthritis, there are countless assistive devices that can make simple tasks easier, but they can be quite costly. The group Makers Making Change has a bank of pre-designed models that are open source and can be 3D printed at a very little cost. My fifth-graders have become very comfortable designing things in Maker's Empire and TinkerCAD through a project where we designed, printed, and sold holiday ornaments to raise money for our local children's hospital. But this idea was so much more than a 3D printing project.

The "4Cs" has been a popular phrase in education for years, recognizing the importance of teaching and allowing the practice of collaboration, critical thinking, communication, and creativity. I believe it is through these "soft skills" that students develop love of learning. Earlier this school year I was invited to take part in a pilot project in my district to explore and implement the ideas of Michael Fullan as outlined in his program, New Pedagogies for Deep Learning. Fullan adds to the 4Cs to include two more: citizenship and character education. Fullan suggests stretching empathy and kindness outside the classroom walls to connect with the community, and how this should be a fundamental aspect of learning. The idea is to emotionally connect students to what they are learning and fill them with purpose. There are countless success stories following his model around the world, it's worth checking out!

During the two weeks we were learning about a variety of physical conditions and we had numerous guests in the classroom.

Parent visitors discussed cystic fibrosis and cerebral palsy, a student's family friend came in to teach us about daily life with rheumatoid arthritis, a representative from the Canadian Arthritis Society and I arranged two Google Hangouts with colleagues at different schools so we could meet their students and find out what kind of devices could help them in their daily lives.

I wanted each group's project to have a person in mind; they weren't just going to make this for anyone, they were making it for someone they have met! As students moved into the research phase, we invited representatives from Brilliant Labs and The Neil Squire Society to help us launch into our prototyping. They showed us more examples of devices that are helpful to people living with specific conditions and we used this as a springboard and inspiration into our own designs.

As expected, the variety of projects were wide and personal. Many students had their family members in mind while designing. Several made devices for people with arthritis, or for the students we met via Google Hangout.

I love maker projects like this because students get to practice the mindset that things can be improved through feedback and trial & error. One group 3D printed a pencil grip design at least eight times to get it right. After all, the goal wasn't just to make a device, it was to make a device that someone in our community could actually use! In the end, we had several devices for holding pencils and markers, a video, fidgets, a cane (3D printed in segments), utensil grips, grocery bag hooks, key holders, a medicine storage container, and even a Micro:Bit proximity sensor to keep someone with vision impairment safe from hazardous areas such as the top of stairs. These 10 and 11-year-olds were learning grade level curriculum that had a greater purpose than anything I've ever been a part of before.

01010010 01101001 01110011 01101011

AUTHENTICITY

Schools don't kill creativity, hierarchies do. Policies do. Compliance does. Outdated systems do. Standardized tests do. Report cards do. Ego does. Competition does. Negativity does. Pressure does. Burnout does. One size fits all methods do. Poor leadership does.

#RiskTakerEdu

Tweet that! Now! Put this down and tweet that!

When I was in tenth-grade, a school project completely changed the trajectory I was on. In fact, I am not even certain I had a path yet, but one was beginning to be carved. A school project that forced me to learn skills as a byproduct of the original process seemed completely relevant and authentic to me. Our task was to construct a posterboard of research around a celebrity. This, after all, was a media studies class. Me, not being much of a cut and paste kind of individual, pitched, à la what we now call Dragon's Den or Shark Tank, a call for action to do more, be more and learn more. I had a small window of opportunity to state my claim and persuade my teacher for buy in. I asked her if I could build a website instead of a posterboard. If you have heard me speak, I tell this story on the regular because I truly believe I am writing this book today as a result of that choice made in 1994. The internet was now mainstream. Google was new. It was exciting. It was exhilarating. Imagine changing code on a screen, hitting refresh, and seeing something immediately come to life. This had never been done before and I wanted to be one of the first to experience it.

So, off I went. Keep in mind I was to be assessed on my research about a celebrity, not my HTML skills or artistic ability to compile a website. Nonetheless, I saw this as an opportunity. If I was going to teach myself HTML, I might as well do it for a school project first!

"Mrs. Boudreau?"
"Yes, Brian?"
"Can I make a website instead of a poster?"
"What is a website??"

I joke but I would love to think that is how the conversation went. As a side, convincing her to build a website instead of a poster was easy. Convincing her of a Tupac fansite? Not so much!

> *If I have learned anything as an educator it is that everyone in my school knows something I don't.*
>
> *#RiskTakerEdu*

When I reflect back, I am reminded of how proud I was of the end result. What started as a school project became something I continued for years to come. A new hobby. A new avenue for learning. I joined other forums that ranked the best fan sites and I was determined to make the top ten list. I met people from all over the world who were also fans of Mr. Shakur. I learned about Flash, a now dated technology. But in those days, if your website had a flash intro, you stood out above the rest. I am getting goosebumps now twenty-six years later remembering how awesome it was to be a member of this online community. Today, everyone has an online community. (If you are not on Twitter, put this down and join immediately. Tweet me, @mraspinall, and I will reply!) But in the mid-nineties, you were fortunate if that was the case. Not only did we collaborate, compete, and share fan art, we learned. We explored. We tested. We remixed. We were a mass not to be messed with. A passionate group of youth celebrating the music of the time by expressing themselves online. It was an extension of ourselves. An accessory, almost like your phone case. We could infer quite a bit about each other just from the color scheme chosen on our website projects. Many stood out on top, but everyone was willing to help.

As with every school project, educators love to brag about the success of their students in the staffroom, and this instance was no different. Mrs. Boudreau was bragging loudly that little Brian Aspinall, a tenth-grade student with Kurt Cobain hair, had successfully built a Tupac Shakur fansite for a school project.

At the time, a good friend of mine was also building a website. However, his choice of action was to create something that didn't depict our high school in a very positive manner. Imagine thinking what you put on the internet would be kept secret?!? That is how early this was in the internet game! Alas, nothing online is secret and a fraudulent bill was sent to the high school in his name. Since he posted the school's address online, it was easily searched. So, the principal eventually found the website and the *charming* adjectives used to describe my friend's experience in high school. Student voice? Sure. Appropriate? No way. My buddy found himself at home for the next few days in full-on suspension mode where he used his time to take down what he had built.

In a fantastic turn of events, and because my principal was a wicked-cool leader, he caught wind of my project and (knowing I was friends with the culprit) turned this into a lesson. I was approached by my principal and asked to build the first-ever Harrow District High School website. He could have asked my friend, but that was the lesson. Use your strengths and skills for good, not evil. I was compensated, my buddy was suspended and we all grew from the experience. But imagine the rapport I now had with my administrator. He became my boss. I made storyboards and graphics and we routinely connected to see if our goals were being met. Imagine building a website, without the consent of IT, because it engaged a student and taught another one about digital citizenship. In fact, I truly believe the rapport my buddy had with this principal also improved as a result. I always thought he might have been a tad jealous. Rightfully so, I guess. His loss was my win.

In my last year as an eighth-grade teacher, I remembered this high school experience and set about getting my students to run our social media for my classroom. Wait, *our* classroom, not mine. Wait, *THEIR* classroom. You know what I mean. It was a risk and many colleagues warned against it. What could go wrong? Inappropriate content posted from Mr. A's class? It was a risk I was willing to take. If I want to model digital citizenship, I'm dropping students into the mix. After requesting permission from parents, we made a plan. We needed a content person, marketing person, photographer, hashtag person, etc. And wouldn't you know, everything we did for this "club" fit exactly with my Language Arts curriculum. We have a Media curriculum too. So our club became teachable moments in many different ways - not just curriculum content, but the soft skills we so heavily preach about these days.

> *"Learn the rules like a pro, so you can break them like an artist."*
>
> *- Pablo Picasso*
> *#RiskTakerEdu*

Back to long-haired, west coast rapper Brian Aspinall. After I completed my high school website, I went on to create more websites for community groups and finally headed off to study Computer Science at the University of Windsor in Ontario, Canada. I was hooked. I loved it. I had found a passion and was beginning to monetize it. All because of that one risk Mrs. Boudreau took on me! What a risk taker she was and I am tremendously grateful to her for that day.

My university experience was much different than my high school experience. Imagine a small-town student living in a mostly white community, moving to the city to enroll in a very in-demand program of study. Computer Science was super hot, and still is today. But at the time, we were all dooms-day prepping for Y2K. If you could turn on a computer, you were hired to try and fix that virus. Moving to the city and entering Computer Science had me immersed in a very diverse student body and it was awesome. New languages, new cultures, new food, new ideas! Prior to my culture shock, I had to interview to get into my program. Let me say that again, I had to interview to get into my program. Why am I repeating that twice? Great question and keep asking why. Why? Because we always use post-secondary school as an excuse to continue to use grades. For me, It was the interview that would make or break me as a future Computer Science student. Secondly, I didn't write exams in my Computer Science courses. Instead, we were asked to solve problems using coding and computer science and everything was open book. We didn't memorize syntax nor were we evaluated on our ability to do so. We were evaluated on our ability to solve problems and graded based on the efficiency of our code. Alas, I may be biased, but I am so done with the excuse of post-secondary as a reason to keep grades. How many of our students will even go that route? I believe our future industry will be made up of freelance work with most working remotely. We must teach our young people to be creative problem solvers who can monetize their passions. Who knows what the jobs of tomorrow will look like. It is our students who will define them based on problems we don't yet know are problems, using technologies that they will invent. Remember, the rate of change today is the slowest it will ever be.

I've written about my uncle Ian before but I never really elaborated on the impact his story had on twenty-something-year-old me studying in university. My uncle studied math and was "the most techie" in his company, if my memory serves me. He took a leadership role in IT and was set the task to help save the business from the devastation Y2K was set to bring. Y2K (Year 2000) was a computer glitch. A bug. In 1999 much of the software being used was written prior. In some cases, decades prior. As such, we, the planet, were not sure if programmers in the seventies and eighties had considered what might happen to the computer system clock at midnight on New Year's Eve in 1999. Would it roll over to the year 2000 or set back to 1900 like the miles on my very first car? If many computer systems did roll back to 1900, it meant for a vast series of crashes and burns. Bank software cannot do transactions in the past! Emails being sent from a hundred years ago? What is happening?!?! I'll never forget the news telling everyone to turn off their computer before midnight as if that might save us all. What would happen when we turned it back on the next day? What a time to be alive!

My uncle Ian set about coding potential solutions to the Y2K bug regardless of whether his system was safe from it or not. Talk about authentic problem solving using coding! Man, I was hooked. I recently spoke to him about Y2K and he was very proud of the code he wrote for his billion-dollar company because they used it for years to come. What an impact! What a game-changer! What a risk taker!

Breaking Barriers With Code!
By Maggie Fay (@maggiefay_)

I've known Maggie for quite sometime via social media and was grateful to get to listen to her give a wicked Ignite Talk recently in the Toronto area. She spoke from the heart about "those" kids (my use of quotations is intentional, as was her talk, in that we both aren't fans of labels). Maggie is a special education teacher in the Toronto, Ontario area and has a passion for equity and inclusion. I recently connected with her again after catching wind of some coding activities she was exploring with her students.

Hi Brian!

I love how your book *Code Breaker* talks about how kids need to know how to communicate their ideas. This really stands out to me as I believe that we all communicate differently. I teach a contained Autism / Developmental Disability Class in Peel and my students are always communicating in different ways. Coding communicates a lot with pictures as do the students in my classroom. My passion is inclusion and how to make other students and adults understand that our label is our name versus the disability that someone has.

For example, it is Johnny not "Autistic Johnny."

I think that coding can be used creatively to bring many students together to work as a team.

Students can learn that we all communicate in various ways and that coding can be the activity that brings different students together. Since coding can be done with or without the use of technology it is easily differentiated.

You mention in *Code Breaker* "this book is about changing how we think about teaching, and that sometimes means learning about new technologies." I think the same applies to teaching students with Autism. We need to change how we think about teaching. Our classroom doors can be welcoming where students can learn that it is not a scary and weird place.

For example, many students love to use iPads and just like other students they are fantastic at navigating them. Since coding uses a lot of photos teachers can collaborate as tech buddies with students in a special education class and teach them that we are all different and communicate in many ways. Students in the special needs class have opportunities to further develop their social skills, as do children in the mainstream. We often forget that inclusion also means to include students that are labeled.

We can use coding to break down attitudinal barriers.

I love your line in *Block Breaker* where you say "instead of focusing on technology or a specific tool, let's focus on our pedagogy." What lens are we teaching the lessons through? Have we thought about everyone in the school or are we assuming certain students cannot be part of a lesson because of the label they have been given that we do not understand. Did we even give the students in our class the option to complete an activity with students that have Autism or do we just assume they don't understand? I look forward to using your book to further inspire more integration amongst all students. Just like Mrs. Boudreau took a chance on you and made an impact let us give all students the opportunity to be inspired by an educator who believes in them.

IMPACT

When kids cheat on assignments it is because they have been taught that grades outweigh the importance of knowing things. We need to fix this.

#RiskTakerEdu

I'll never forget seeing an eighth-grade student being dropped off at school by her dad in his eighteen-wheeler on a snow day. Buses had been cancelled due to inclement weather, but she insisted on coming, even though I posted all of our assignments on Google Classroom. There were never any secrets, we adopted a bit of a flipped classroom model and I immediately stopped getting asked "what are we doing today?" as soon as the first bell rang. But why was this student at school? In fact, why were ninety percent of our students at school? Our seventh and eighth graders never came to school on snow days, so what was happening?

"FOMO," they said.
"FOMO?" I asked.
"Fear of missing out."
"But all the assignments are posted online."
"Mr. A, it isn't about the assignments."

We can use Learning Management Systems to teach content until we are blue in the face. But the in-person conversations, rapport, recess breaks, and laughter...well, you need to be at school for that. We knew we were doing something right. My students had successfully posted on social media that buses were cancelled without me approving the post (gradual release of responsibility) but nonetheless, they all showed up!

However, impact can lead to very toxic cultures as well. Twenty-something-year-old Brian Aspinall was a Tupac and Biggie Smalls fan in his university days and I will never forget hearing *Juicy* for the first time. While the lyrics are too much for this book, I'll simply quote the first line of one of Notorious B.I.G's most successful songs.

"Yeah, this album is dedicated
To all the teachers that told me I'd never amount to nothin"

Not how I want to be remembered!

Christopher Wallace, aka Biggie Smalls aka The Notorious B.I.G. hated school so much he dropped out and dedicated his first smash hit to those naysayers. Teacher naysayers. Teachers who wrote him off from the beginning. Teachers who didn't care. Teachers who likely never knew about his music and art nor cared enough to even ask.

> *The best educators don't put others down but instead find comfort in lifting them up. We are better together.*
>
> *#RiskTakerEdu*

Our impact, good or bad, will leave lasting impressions. Kids will forget dates and formulas, but they will never forget who you are as an individual. I don't demand respect, I earn it. This isn't my classroom or my school, it is ours. It is yours.

"Don't friend students on social media!" they said.

Why not? I did. I still do. In fact, many of my former students are now parents with successful jobs and I followed the entire journey on Instagram. Many of my former students have written to me on those platforms thanking me for taking risks on them. In fact, I have had students congratulate *me* on those platforms for my body of work. Imagine that. Former students, proud of their former teacher because we are able to stay connected. Still a rapport, all these years later. I believe strongly in the importance of transparency. If students can see my personal life, they can connect with me, much like I can connect with them. Just yesterday, a colleague's student showed me a video of his new chickens because he knew I had chickens as well after seeing it online.

While dates and formulas are important, access to information has never been greater and what we choose to do with new information makes all the difference. Students who feel valued and trusted will outperform those who do not. Program determines behavior. Compliance doesn't have to mean quiet rows. It can be engagement. It can mean investment. It should be about trust, not fear. It should be about honesty, not deceit. We used to attend school because that is where the knowledge was. Being educated meant knowing a lot of things. To me, being educated means knowing enough to find resources, people, places and things in order to solve real problems.

What happened to Biggie Smalls is very unfortunate, being gunned down in his twenties. Kudos to him for building a short but tremendous career around his passions. Kudos to him for leaving a toxic environment and chasing his dreams. Perhaps just one small act of kindness at his high school and he might still be alive. One positive community group for him to feel safe to share his ideas and his outcome might have been different. He didn't know anything other than negative community groups, and he rapped about it and it cost him his life. His story has had a tremendous impact on me, initially as a fan, but even more so now as an educator. I never want to be rapped about like that. I never want to be remembered like that.

Finding Fitness
By Nicole Kaufman (@Teach_MsK)

All too often we, as teachers, focus on the mental health of our students. We make sure our classrooms are inclusive, safe, communities where students are encouraged to try their best, make mistakes and go through positive struggle. They have an outlet to discuss their struggles and we keep an eye on students who may be dealing with mental health issues on a daily basis. But our own mental health is sometimes pushed to the side, because we should be old enough to deal with it and know what to do. Let me tell you firsthand, this is not always the case. We know what it is like to deal with unhappy days, days where we are celebrating, and days that you just wish the stress would end. What do we do? Anything? Do we keep it bottled up or do you let it out in some way? What is your outlet, when life is just not going in a forward direction? For me, it was fitness.

Let me paint you a picture. Four years ago, I lost over fifty pounds. My class was super supportive, we did workouts together, they checked in and we were in a great place. I was in a great place. A first time contract teacher, a supportive class and a fabulous support system. Fast forward a year, an injury, little motivation, putting the weight back on and well, you have a very unhappy, unmotivated, lethargic Nicole. I wasn't happy, and this took a toll on my job, and the rapport I had in the classroom. How could I expect my students to work to their full potential when I wasn't able to lead by example? Forward two more years and here I am, pursing fitness as my outlet for stress, and to keep my mental health in check. Everything from Personal Training, Swimming, Yoga, Cross-fit and Running help to create a mindset where I believe and am confident in who I am as a person. Having goals, reaching them, making new ones, struggling but still moving forward go hand in hand with changing mindset and the knowledge that things do take time. Fitness and this general way of thinking has become part of my daily life and a way for me to focus on myself outside of teaching.

Going beyond extra curricular for me, fitness then became something that was brought into the school day. I was open with students about my goals and my past, and they started noticing a difference in me as a person and a teacher both mentally and physically. We did weekly workouts together, sometimes crammed in the classroom, other times outdoors on our school property. As with any activity, you get the students who are in it with you, they want to ask questions, they keep you accountable, and then you get the ones who just do the minimum work requirement to get through the process. For me personally, this was a way to stay accountable and show students that goal setting doesn't just get accomplished over night.

I think the biggest moment I've had with my students was in 2018 at Bark Lake Leadership Centre. It was here that I totally realized the impact of everything that I had accomplished the year before. I was always very timid about doing high ropes courses, because of so many different factors. This time, I put trust in my friend Sandra when she told me that I could do it. Changing my mindset was a huge factor to go along with my physical ability to climb. That day was one I will never forget. I made it to the top of the Pamper Pole. I used skills from the gym to take full advantage of my legs to help push me up the course. Inspiring students in the process. This year again, Sandra and I, as well as one of my grade 8 students took on the challenge of the Aspire Tower. Again, mindset along with physical ability was what pushed us to the top! It wasn't easy and I can say with certainty that there were moments I didn't think I could continue but having a teammate forced me to dig deep, trust in the ropes team and the skills that I held.

In my situation, one of the biggest keys is staying accountable. Whether it is students commenting on my healthy lunch, to them questioning a treat I decide to eat. Staff members who have also made healthy life changes and are involved in fitness as well. We became a group of people who have made the decision to focus on our mental health in a way that promotes a healthy lifestyle. My mental well being is 100 percent impacted by having a team of people who I trust, that help me chase excellence in this journey. Having a team to keep me accountable allows me a much needed break from the pressures that we teachers sometimes find ourselves in.

On my own, the gym is my playground and my safe place to leave behind the stresses of the day. At home, books and podcasts are ways that I learn new things, educate myself and think about what comes next. How do you focus on your mental and physical health when it comes to your chosen profession? I would love to hear about your journey, too!

Determination

You never learn anything from being perfect. Mistakes are a big part of the process.

#RiskTakerEdu

I was originally naming this chapter *Failure* but instead went with *Determination*.

Why? Great question.

Failure, in the context of school, is very bad. Failure means repeating things. Do-overs. Fix this. Do that. I would never want to repeat a process without any feedback as to why I am doing so. Determination, on the other hand, can be related to failure, but through a more positive lens. Rovio was determined to be successful when they built their fifty-second app called Angry Birds. Yes, fifty-second app. To them, failing fifty-one times prior was a learning experience, not defeat. And now we have 17 different Angry Birds apps, board games, a cartoon series and major motion pictures. They "failed" 51 times. That list doesn't sound like failure to me. That is determination, grit, and perseverance and I'd love to learn more about their six-year process!

Determination, or the firmness of purpose, is something I want all students to experience. But it does come with a catch. In fourth-grade I was very determined to complete my word searches in the shortest amount of time. Why? Because we were rewarded with candy for doing so. Let me say that again, I was given candy for finishing my word search in the shortest amount of time. I was determined to get that candy. However, many of my peers were not.

Why? Because they didn't think they stood a chance to win. In essence, the fun of a word search had been completely sucked out of the activity because of the competitive nature of the task. We were not being graded, but we were being rewarded. Instead of an A, I got Smarties. I was determined. But many were not. I cannot remember learning anything other than strategies to complete word searches. I couldn't even tell you the theme of the words. But the strategy was simple. Start with the top row. Scan left to right, look for patterns and vowels. Check the four corners on the diagonal. Once you found a word on the horizontal, start looking vertically as they often cross each other. You get the idea. I don't remember the content, but I was killer at the word search game!

> *We should celebrate our colleague's successes as much as we do our student's successes. Collaboration, not competition.*
>
> *#RiskTakerEdu*

I ran a gradeless classroom for years and always dealt with the "what about report cards?" question. Report cards? Pfft. Who cares?! In a twenty-first century classroom with great pedagogy, report cards are redundant. Everything has been communicated already with Google, SeaSaw, Flipgrid, etc. There are no secrets. There is transparency. If parents are hearing about a child's progress for the first time from the report card, we have a major problem. And no one reads them anyway so stop stressing over writing them. In fact, they should already be written. Simply copy and paste the learning goals from your <Insert App Name> and voila. Done. Report cards are a thing of the past, as are grades. Feedback is the new grades. Feedback keeps kids moving. Feedback keeps staff moving. Feedback keeps parents moving. Feedback helped the Raptors win the NBA title.

Being determined forces us to redefine what it means to fail at school. When students are determined to solve problems for local community groups, there is no failure. Only bumps in the road to victory with a positive, genuine impact on both student learning and community values. Failure, in a school context, has always meant a student did not get a high enough score for a variety of reasons. Not knowing content? Maybe. Not applying knowledge? Sure. Not having breakfast? Likely. Being up all night because of <insert family problems here>. Definitely! It is not easy being a kid these days and those determined enough to come to school should be celebrated. If kids come late, thank them for being there rather than punish for tardiness. If your students continuously ask you "what did I get?" they are determined to get the mark, not learn something new. If they are asking about grades, their definition of failure is not the same as mine. I have failed many times. I am a computer programmer by trade and programs never work properly the first time through. But I am always determined to fix the problem. Debug the bug. Create a solution. When kids are determined to achieve a grade, they are constantly looking for answers instead of creating solutions to authentic problems. If your student body has a goal to raise $5000 for a community group but only reaches $2500, that is not failure. That is success. Think about your next math task. Failure should not be about getting answers wrong, but about blips on the radar while travelling through the creative and constructive process.

Redefining failure will have a tremendous positive impact on your class community. Traditionally, when kids fail, they are often kept in at recess. Let us dissect this bit. Ultimately the goal is to help students but you are just taking your time and their opportunity to blow off energy and steam. Recess should be a mandatory part of every student's day and never removed for punishment. It should never be used as a reward either because it sends a message that recess is a privilege, not a right.

> *When kids write code, it typically does not work properly the first time. This is a good thing. This is where learning begins. This is where problem solving begins. This is where innovation begins.*
>
> *#RiskTakerEdu*

Determination will yield new conversations.

"I believe in you."
"You can do this."
"I know it seems difficult but I can help."
"I believe in you."

Biggie Smalls felt written off and created his own destiny. This will not be the case for everyone. Many students who feel written off and drop out may never know what it feels like to be considered successful. Ironically in these cases, it is school that has failed them.

Empower Our Girls!
By Daphne McMenemy (@McMenemyTweets)

I saw a tweet recently by Jay Flores (@JayFlores2032) that read, "My biggest fear is that the cure to cancer is trapped in the mind of a young girl who is told that STEM is for boys". This sparked a conversation between a colleague and I about our experiences with STEM at school and gender stereotypes. In the end we were both in agreement that while our current experiences with STEM at the primary level don't scream Boys Only or Girls Don't Belong, somewhere down the line girls are receiving that very message. I continue to read research about the number of girls versus boys in computer science classes in high school and at the post-secondary level and that STEM careers continue to be dominated by men. This research and these statistics always have me reflecting on the messages I convey, both verbally and non-verbally, as a teacher, as a mother, and how these messages were conveyed to me throughout my childhood and what I did with them.

Growing up in the 80s and 90s I was always called a tomboy – a term I grew to loathe. I liked baggy clothes and hated dresses. I could spend my days playing baseball and video games, making crafts and playing with Barbies. I did not fully understand why this was a problem, but it was, and it defined who I thought I was. But the more I heard, "That's for boys…" or "This isn't for girls…" the more I pushed back. I liked doing those things, and why should I have to stop? I grew up across decades that had very clear definitions of what girls did and what boys did. My likes and dislikes didn't fit in just one category; I sat nicely in the middle. Fast-forward thirty years - I grew up and still sit nicely in the middle of those not so clearly defined categories anymore. And now I'm raising a little girl who is just like me, in a tinier package. She loves Ninja Turtles and fancy dresses. She spends her days crafting, making, coding and rock climbing. She picks up bugs and draws chalk rainbows on the sidewalk. She is not defined as a tomboy, she is celebrated for being true to herself.

People often think that the first step in conquering these stereotypes starts with boys - that our girls are being told they can't or shouldn't by the males in their lives. The truth of it is they're wrong. Sure, there are boys who believe girls can't play hockey or pink is a "girl colour", but in my experience, those that had the biggest issue and the most to say about who I was when I was growing up were the girls and women in my life. Even today, as a mother, I hear two comments, "She's such a cool girl" and "She likes boy things". The latter from the girls and the former from the boys.

Just like her, I was given so many different opportunities to decide who I wanted to be. Although my mom wished just a little (maybe slightly more than a little) that I'd want to wear a tutu and jump around in a ballet class, she bought me my first ball glove and cheered the loudest in the bleachers at every game. Every little girl deserves every opportunity to make her own decisions about who she is and who she wants to be.

Jay's post made me realize the importance of empowering my little girl, and every little girl I teach to be exactly who they are; to be defined not by gender stereotypes but by the joy and love they approach life with. As a teacher I strive every day to give all of my students opportunities to explore their world in different ways – ways that make them think, ways that make them question. If we don't give our kids these opportunities, how will they ever know? We need to empower our little girls to change gender stereotypes, to break molds, to define themselves in whichever ways they want. We need to empower them to question, to think, to be bold and brave. We need to empower them to change the research and make their own statistics.

UNAFRAID

"Confront the dark parts of yourself, and work to banish them with illumination and forgiveness. Your willingness to wrestle with your demons will cause your angels to sing."

- August Wilson
#RiskTakerEdu

When I first went into education, I found it incredibly overwhelming. There were report card rules I knew nothing about, but not written down anywhere for anyone to find. I didn't know what I had to report on, how often I had to report it, and if I had to fill comment boxes completely with educational jargon that parents wouldn't ever understand.

But let us back this horse up. I had to learn curriculum. I had to teach curriculum. I didn't know from year-to-year if and what grade I might have to teach next year due to having little seniority. I was nervous. I was scared. It was so bad I wore dark clothes to hide the sweat marks every single day and spent my prep and lunchtimes trying to dry my clothes under the dryer in the bathroom. I was embarrassed that I didn't know what I didn't know and I didn't feel I could ask anyone. I felt supply teaching was very competitive. It was all in who you knew and I knew nobody. I wasn't from there. But I also knew I wanted a contract teaching job so I worked myself silly. Countless hours as if seeing my car still in the parking lot at 7:00 pm made me a good teacher.

People will notice, I thought.

Wrong.

Well, they did notice, and reminded me to go home and get some rest.

But I needed a job!

"How do you ever expect kids to listen to you when you dress like them?" I was told in my first year.

It really threw me for a loop. If teaching meant I had to wear a tie, I was out. After all, I played in the gym and crawled on the floor like they did too. At the time, my feelings were really hurt. I even bought a new wardrobe. But the truth of the matter is, my classroom wasn't built on hierarchy. My style was different and that was OK. We weren't the same person, so why would we think similarly. That's what makes having colleagues awesome. Assuming we aren't tearing each other down. When I heard that comment shouted to me from the doorway as I sat at my teacher desk, I immediately knew it would resurface in the staffroom so I avoided that place too. What a shame!

I worry that we don't care as much about staff well-being as we do student well-being. Something about being an adult makes it acceptable to live in pain. To live in fear. To feel judged. To feel inadequate. The daily pressures of working in education are ridiculously exhausting and the gossip that arises when people take "sick" days makes me sick. Mental health days are important. Mental health days are crucial. Mental health days are required. If we want kids to do their best, we must also be at our best. Never feel guilty for taking a break. Trust me, I know you have more than earned it.

I was ecstatic when I landed my first teaching gig, a fifth-grade position, around Spring Break my first year out of school. I had spent September through March supply teaching and building as many relationships as I could while sacrificing my own back at home. I was willing to drive as far as our school board was large geographically. The more people I knew, the more supply days I might get and eventually sign that permanent contract!

Luckily it all worked out in the end, but the stress and pressure never went away. In fact, it grew. Now I had a job. Now I was responsible for a full year of young adults. I was responsible for permission slips, lunch money, school sports, yearbook, seating plans, lesson plans, marking, re-marking, conferencing, etc. etc. I don't need to remind you! If you look at my first few class photos from back then, you will notice me attempting to lean forward slightly, elbows pressed into my stomach, attempting to hide any sweat marks I knew the camera would find. Today, I speak to thousands of parents, students, and teachers across North America and I still sweat. I'm still a nervous wreck every time. A basket of anxiety waiting to be spilled into the audience. But I think this is important as it means I care. I care about my students. I care about the teachers I teach. I care about the audience I want to inspire. I want to amplify teacher voice in order to amplify student voice. You may have noticed some wicked contributions right here in this book.

I will never forget the first time a student noticed me sweating and proceeded to make sure every else noticed too. This lead to me getting angry and embarrassed, in which case, I lost my temper rather than speak my truth. As we went down this spiral of emotions, it was apparent I was insecure. I'm sure my students thought so too. After all, everyone knew I had zero experience. I even remember a parent stepping in during a basketball practice because I had lost control of the team. Imagine that!

But where was I to turn for assistance? I had close teacher friends who would understand but I wanted someone with experience to guide me. Unfortunately, I was afraid that admitting I needed help in the classroom management department would lead me to finding a new school and a different grade. Why does the staffroom have to be so toxic? We are teammates, remember?

That first year was an incredible whirlwind. I cried often, thinking I wasn't meant to teach. This made me

sweat more and feel more insecure. It was cyclical and I didn't know what to do.
But it wasn't all negative. In fact, what came of that first year set me on the path I am on today.

That first year, I was introduced to Scratch by my seventh- and eighth-grade students. You know that now-famous coding program? That one. It was originally built in 2002.

Picture me, jumping for joy about this *new* coding tool with six-inch diameter sweat marks under my armpits. I no longer cared. I found it. This was the tool that was going to change everything. As you know, I was a Computer Science major before going into education. I found my niche using coding to teach my curriculum right from my first year, all thanks to those students who made the now-infamous Pooping Baby Game.

I played with Scratch at home often. I revelled at the simple interface, made coding commands without writing syntax and immediately recognized a plethora of curriculum connections. I was hooked. I was excited!

Teachers teach to their strengths. I think this is a good thing for a variety of reasons. First, we get passionate about the things we enjoy and that energy is contagious. Second, we expose students to things they might not regularly see. In this case, coding. But coding wasn't as popular then as it is today. In fact, it wasn't really anything unless you were directly related to Computer Science.

I remember heading to the computer lab with a handful of kids, eager to finally get my opportunity to shine. To be noticed. To be engaging. To be less sweaty.

In those days, Scratch was a download. It didn't run in the browser like it does today. This proved problematic. For starters, we didn't have computer permissions with our accounts to install anything on the computers in the lab and secondly, USB ports were blocked so no one could upload a virus.

I remember thinking to myself, I need to do this. I need to get this program onto these computers because I know it will be a game changer for me, and them. I will ask for forgiveness rather than ask for permission. This is my chance. I asked my posse of kids if they could beat the USB firewall because I knew a workaround with the installation part. As we closed the door and dimmed the lights for true stealth mode, we became a team. Rebels. Risk takers. Coders. Learners. Adventurers. We made a train of people to get the install done as soon as possible and hid the Scratch icon so as to go unnoticed. Think

Ocean's Eleven, but with twelve-year-olds. We were on fire!

And done. Success!

I went home that night thinking one of two things.

This is going to be epic.

Or,

I am never getting a job now.

See, I had broken a few rules to allow the "Poop" Storm game to be built. Every time a student called it Poop Storm they would wink at me as if I didn't know what they really called the game when I wasn't around. Looking back, the whole thing was a giant shit storm but I am forever grateful for those moments as they left a lasting impact on me as an educator and sent me down the constructivist path I am still on today. But more than me, those kids mastered the Cartesian Plane without any explicit teaching. They knew which integer signs put Sprites in which corners. They had demonstrated a mastery of Geometry and I was left thinking about how to evaluate it. Grades. Ugh. They mastered it. I watched it happen. No test. No paper. No fear. They took risks, collaborated, and without realizing it, taught me a

great deal about teaching, learning and myself.
Suddenly, I found myself sweating less.

Chasing Greatness
By Don Epps (@DonEppsEDU)

People ask me, "What are you are trying to accomplish as a leader, or basically what's your endgame?" I tell them that I'm on a relentless mission to Close the Caring Gap! I'm trying to help people care about something bigger than themselves! I'm trying to inspire people to unleash their passion and purpose about what they are here on this planet to do! This can happen in any walk of life. In education, I want our kids to come every day to a learning experience, where they care about getting out of that car or off that bus racing in the front door excited to be at school! I want teachers on fire to be at school ready to make a positive difference every day! That's what it is all about; it's not complicated: if you care you have purpose, you have passion and you have pride! I will continue to say this over and over again so let's not make this concept of caring complicated!

True game changers in education are fearless about going outside the box to bring the absolute best learning experience to their students! I refuse to worry about what people might think when taking risks as an educational disruptor but rather what kind of impact that decision will have on the people I serve! I lead with a relentless commitment of serving others in how I would want to be led; treating people the right way never goes out of style. In becoming a principal, I believed in converting my classroom culture to an entire building. I swore to myself that when I became an administrator I would never change what made me a difference-maker as a teacher and a coach! I am on a mission to create a learning experience that the students can't imagine missing, building a culture that kids never want to leave: a school culture that reaches new heights through a shared vision of growing lifelong learners and where our teachers feel supported to take the top off the learning experience.

Learning environments thrive where failure is not feared but rather is an opportunity to grow. It's ok to have fun and be real with the ones you serve! Be authentic because if you pose as something you're not the kids and teachers will read right through you, inhibiting any trust from being formed! Being called an educational disruptor is one of the biggest compliments I have been given as a principal! I reject the status quo! I refuse to be average for the kids and teachers I serve; they deserve the best. I will do whatever it takes to connect and build relationships with the people I serve! If this means making goofy YouTube videos, giving a Ric Flair WOO in a class that I'm observing when greatness is on display or doing the splits at assemblies, I'm all in. That's who I am: I'm an authentic dork and proud of it! Great leaders are defined by the culture of the whole organization they lead not the ego of one! Educational leaders who are unwilling to release power to their staff will alienate their teachers, stunting a high performance learning environment. Encourage strategic risk taking to assure best practice collides with next practice.

Promote a growth mindset culture where there is never an endgame but rather a growth game! Bestselling author Jim Collins says, "Good is the enemy of GREAT." I consider good to be gateway drug to average, and there is nothing average in what we are trying to accomplish for the kids we serve as educators. I've learned throughout my life that people are not inspired by your looks or the sound of your voice. They are truly inspired by your passion for life and your ability to care for others! A true inspiration sparks greatness in others!

A true inspiration motivates you to strive to be the best you! A true inspiration pushes you to the limits of your potential! That's what the mission of #ChasingGreatness is all about in the relentless pursuit of being the best version of YOU! This drives my mission of doing whatever it takes to make a positive difference in the lives of the ones I serve. Let's make a difference together, be the difference every day in every way for not only the ones served but for yourself because you deserve it!

HONESTY

"Integrity is telling myself the truth. And honesty is telling the truth to other people."

- *Spencer Johnson*
#RiskTakerEdu

I wanted to end that last chapter on a positive note. But I do need to be truthful to myself. I have struggled with depression. I have struggled with anxiety. I have struggled with burnout. I have taken medications. I have sought professional help. This is the first time I have put something like this in print. My family doesn't even know the truth. So why here?

I'm tired.
I'm tired of teacher bashing.
I'm tired of name-calling.
I'm tired of the judgment.
I'm tired of never feeling adequate.

We are better together. We need to work together. We need to help each other. We need to lead each other. Squad goals. Cherish your teammates.

Teacher burnout is real. I've seen it. I've lived it. I've felt it. Imagine the impact this leaves on our classrooms and schools. So why suggest so-and-so just can't cut it rather than try to offer a helping hand to that colleague? Behavior is a form of communication.

Moving forward, I promise to never gossip, never intimidate, and never undermine any staff member I am working with. A toxic school community does nothing but hurt the kids who have no choice but to attend there. And who knows what their home life looks like.

Begin each day lifting up two other people. Notice how contagious that gesture will be. Kids will notice, staff will notice and parents will notice. Lifting others up will lift you up. You will feel better. You will be better. Your students will feel better. Your students will be better.

Next school year, prompt your colleagues with a simple Google Form.

"What is your name and what is your favorite treat?"

Surprise them throughout the year when they are in a funk. The simplest gestures often leave the biggest impacts. The same goes for our students. When someone is acting out, offer them a treat, a hand, and a listening ear. Listen to their words, not just to respond. Get to know them. Understand them. Talk about stuff not related to school. Relationships matter most.

While great leadership plays a role, we cannot point fingers at anyone but ourselves. When we make others better, we make ourselves better. We are better together.

Being Mr. Coder Guy, I've heard countless times from educators that they "are not as techie" as I am. So? What *are* you good at? Find it. Cherish it. Share it. Scream it! Coding is a thing of today and like most tools, may not be the thing of tomorrow. But you will be. You will still be here. It is the classroom memories that matter most and I want you to create them, share them and scream them for all to hear. You matter. Our kids matter. Be honest with yourself.

Being honest with yourself and modelling it is the best way for kids to follow suit. Kids are dishonest out of fear of punishment. We can love and discipline kids without punishing. Discipline and punishment are not the same thing. Discipline means to help alter behavior in accordance with regulations while punishment attempts to inflict suffering as a result of bad behavior. I'll argue that discipline builds rapport and punishment kills it. Don't be a rapport killer. I once was. Nothing good came from it.

Flexible Seating is Flexible Thinking
By Laura Kennedy (@Lkennedy37)

I have always liked finding a cozy little nook to make my own. Think of that extra end on a row, corner spot on a sectional or a tree branch bowed outward creating a little hideaway spot. My school days however, were spent predominantly in regimental rows. I remember specifically when desks were arranged into groups of four. It was a different perspective and one that gave a new flow and mood to the room. It was short lived of course because it did not allow for complete control at the front of the room.

When I began substitute teaching I was bound by the set up of the teacher and wouldn't dream of disturbing the organization. It did give me a wide perspective of how and why set up is an important factor. Furniture and space can dictate how a day goes and subsequently the learning. When I was given a longer stint in the class, I quickly realized who could use a break from sitting next to each other so the dance of the desks began. Multiply that a number of times and you have the makings of a workout video. Putting name tags on velcro strips made for easier movement until I realized that claiming a desk for the year was like an explorer 'discovering' new land and was unnecessary.

Banging into corners of the desks gave me visions of bringing in a band saw to make everything rounded. This began my search of organizational strategies and rolling carts was the starting point. Think about how we feel in close public spaces such as on airplanes, movie theatres or elevators. When we are crammed in, we aren't necessarily bringing our best selves to the moment. With space and alternate places to choose, our interactions can rise to the occasion.

Upon getting my own room, the sleeves were rolled up and blueprints were drawn. Constantly observing how students interacted with each other had me switching things around as if the class was on a big roulette wheel.

At first students were all a-twitter when they came in the next day to see everything changed around. They came to recognize that the space was what it was - an area where we work. It felt like a page out of Dr. Suess - we work here, we work there, on the floor, by the door, in a group, with some soup (just needed a rhyme for that last one!) The message is that you work where you need to productively, and allow others to do what they need in their space.

The best compliment I received was that I couldn't be found in the class when a visitor popped their head in the door. They soon came to realize that I was most often on the floor with the students listening, building and connecting. If that eye level meant a worm's eye view, that was us lying stomach down sharing what we were doing in a circle, tossing dice or number markers into the middle and rolling something around the room. How else do you curl 3-D shapes, see how many milliliters are in a graduated cylinder or read? You definitely cannot do any of this with desks in the way lined up in regimental rows.

I began with one yoga ball for a particular student with a developmental need. Other students expressed interest in having the yoga ball as a chair so the quick solution was to rotate it throughout the room. I posted a class roster which the students organized the schedule. The hunt for all types of furniture, particularly on wheels became my focus. Enter the term, "Flexible Seating." Well shiver my timbers, it has a name! I saw a few posts on my Twitter feed and was drawn to them like a magnet. Kayla Delzer's post began my formal introduction to this concept and what a guru to follow. Her connection to the Starbucks model resonated with me.

Somehow the college student, aspiring writer, parent with strollers and business associates all work and co-exist in the same space. Tables of different heights, couches, benches and shelf space to lean on, place a drink and charge devices can all be found in the same space.

Being able to move items to accommodate the particular group is what allows them to co-exist in the same space.

I was fortunate to win a rolling chart stand and offered a few items to get started on our flexible classroom journey. The day our standing table arrived from Trade West, the students literally hugged it and made instant use by standing at and under it at the same time. The beauty of this journey is that free items can be easily gathered and used immediately. Students have used milk crates to make makeshift office areas, stacked them and used cushions to create instant seats.

On the first day I had NO set up. I had students scan the room to see the different options and showed them how to create a blueprint. Armed with grid paper, they drew shapes to represent the furniture and then taped them to the page. We shared our visions for what the room could be. Prior to the end of day bell in the last few weeks, I invited students to find partners to choose an item to move. Standing to the side watching this collaboration was to witness a choreographed ballet the likes that even Twyla Tharp could never have imagined. Instead of being miffed that others weren't doing it right or impeding on each others' space, the students moved with precision and purpose to create the space. It goes to prove that when involved, a group can be trusted; or rather relied upon to work productively for the benefit of all.

Imagine that; all just because of one yoga ball. The 'exercise' of trying one thing leads to the strength of practice, flexibility and the power of purpose.

PERSEVERANCE

"I finally realized that I must do my schoolwork to keep from being ignorant, to get on in life, to become a journalist, because that's what I want! I know I can write ..., but it remains to be seen whether I really have talent …"

- Anne Frank
#RiskTakerEdu

Kids these days. Amiright? Boy. What has the world become? OK, I kid. Satire. I couldn't put together a book about nonconformists without mentioning those changing the world right now, could I? Many have rocked the boat before us, and many will after our time. But let us take a moment and celebrate those brilliant young minds who are making the world a better place.

Malala Yousafzai was fourteen when she was shot in the head while riding a school bus. An activist, Yousafzai, at the age of only eleven, gained notoriety after writing about Pakistani life under the Taliban rule. Not before long, she was on the speaking circuit encouraging girls to fight for their right to education. After surviving the assassination, she went on to win a Nobel Peace Prize in 2014, the youngest person ever to do so.

"Since our leaders are behaving like children, we will have to take the responsibility they should have taken long ago. We have to understand what the older generation has dealt to us, what mess they have created that we have to clean up and live with. We have to make our voices heard."

- Greta Thunberg
#RiskTakerEdu

Greta Thunberg is a Swedish teen activist who has become a leading voice for climate change activism. Since 2018, over one million students have joined her in walking out of their classrooms to protest no action on climate change.

Greta has been very open about life with autism and has used it to help shape her activism which is inspiring to me. We all have opportunity with proper access, and can make our voices heard if we choose to do so.

> "This award is not just for me. It is for those forgotten children who want education. It is for those frightened children who want peace. It is for those voiceless children who want change. I am here to stand up for their rights, to raise their voice. It is not time to pity them."
>
> - Malala Yousafzai
> #RiskTakerEdu

Xiuhtezcatl Martinez is another environmental activist who, before he was even fifteen, spoke three times at the U.N. He is among twenty-two people around his age involved with a lawsuit against their federal government suggesting that the right to life, liberty, and property is being affected by climate change. In 2015, his hip-hop song *Speak For the Trees* was selected as the theme song for the United Nations Climate Change Conference.

Iqbal Masih was just ten years old when he broke free from slavery and quickly became a leader in the movement helping thousands of children escape bondage. He travelled the globe speaking about his activism but, unfortunately, was assassinated at the young age of twelve. After a massive funeral on his behalf, Congress started an annual award given to other activists fighting to end child labor.

Kids these days. How crazy is it to think young people leaving a global mark become targets by groups looking to shut them down. True heroes, advocating for their beliefs on a global scale before entering adulthood. These are only a few stories of the many found online. I think it is important for our students to be exposed to such stories. We don't expect all of our students to make a global impact, but one small change in their own community makes all the difference in many peoples' lives.

Many of these young activists have TEDx Talks. Show them to your students. Discuss them with your students. Infer and explore what it might be like to be them, living in different countries and facing different fears. Fire up the Google Street View and have a look at their communities. What do you think they eat? How do you think they dress? What might the weather be like? Draw upon your Language Arts curriculum. Draw upon your Geography curriculum. Draw upon your History curriculum. There are multiple connections to existing curriculum when discussing these stories. In fact, have students blog about their own experiences, failures, and successes. Be transparent. Persevere through the tough times.

I do want to share one more story because of the STEAM nature of the invention. Remember, our students will solve problems in their world that we do not yet recognize as problems, using technologies they will invent. Ann Makosinski invented a flashlight powered by body heat when she was just fifteen years old. Her invention provides light to those who cannot afford electricity while limiting battery waste. Ann also created the eDrink, which takes excess heat from a hot beverage and charges your devices. As a result of her awesomeness, she had acquired several brand partnerships and even appeared on the Tonight Show.

Kids these days. Amiright?

Disrupting the Perception of Discipline
By Joshua Stamper (@Joshua__Stamper)

We had a student ask their teacher for permission to go to the nurse because he had a headache. As the student entered the nurses office, the nurse immediately saw the student did not have a pass and told him to go back to class. As the student was leaving the nurse's office, two teachers stopped the student in the hallway and, very loudly, demanded for the student to go back to class. The student complied and went back to class to retrieve a pass from his teacher. When the student came back with a pass to the nurse, the same two teachers stood in front of the door, stopped him, and told the student to go back to class. When the student became visibly and verbally upset, I was called to come to the nurse's office to assist. When I arrived, all parties had elevated emotions and everyone was yelling. I calmly asked for the student to come to my office. The student agreed to walk to my office and the two teachers began to follow us. As I turned around, the student kept repeating to the two teachers, "please go away and stop yelling at me." Before the teachers could enter my office, I told them I had everything under control and I shut my office door. I could tell the teachers were frustrated at the outcome but I was trying to de-escalate the situation quickly. This student had a history of trauma and he did not possess the needed skills to control his emotions. I knew the result was going to be unrecoverable if I let the dialog continue. After using several de-escalation strategies, the student was able to calm down and reflect on the entire event, which included how he could have improved his interaction with the teachers.

The next day, I met with everyone involved to discuss what occurred and to establish a protocol for the future. The teachers were upset because I shut my office door on them and they weren't involved in the discipline process. The perception was that the student didn't receive a harsh enough punishment and the student should have received In-School Suspension (ISS). It was evident there was a misperception of discipline.

I asked the teachers, "How many times has this student been to ISS this year?"

The response was, "Often."

"Has the punishment worked?"

The teachers did not respond but it was evident they understood my point.

During my career as an administrator, I have seen many staff members yell at a student to correct their behavior. The assumption is that the student will respond in a compliant and respectful manner. However, in my experience, at the middle school level students often respond by talking back, walking away from the teacher, or shutting down completely (fight/flight/freeze).

Childhood trauma is one of the greatest components our educators face today. Based on the Adverse Childhood Experience (ACE) data, 67% of our population has experienced at least one form of trauma and the numbers are only increasing. It's imperative we focus on the social-emotional needs of our students to combat the negative experiences they are facing elsewhere.

If our mindset is that each child has experienced trauma, our techniques and strategies are going to be vastly different. The results of negative interaction will not change unless we, as educators, change our mindsets and use our trauma-informed strategies to interact with our students. When students have large emotions, which result in big behaviors, we must model composure not mirror chaos.

Negative behavior is a symptom of a larger problem, which is deeply rooted in our student's social and emotional health. We can not assume that each child understands or knows how to interact appropriately with adults or authority figures. Behavior is a form of communication. If we view behavior in this way, instead of a personal quality, effectively decoding misbehavior will help us determine the child's unmet need. We cannot enhance learning without improving the emotional wellbeing of the heart.

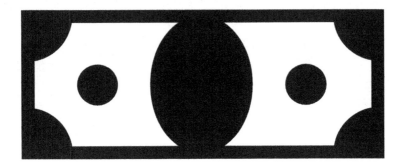

CHANGE

Never forget you are not JUST a teacher. You are not JUST the math teacher. You are not JUST the art teacher. You are not JUST the phys. ed. teacher. You are not JUST the history teacher. You are a professional educator who cares! The system NEEDS YOU and so do our kids!

#RiskTakerEdu

Today's smartphones are not a result of continued improvement to the telegraph. At some point, an entirely new system needed to be created which made the previous one obsolete. Brands that stand out do so because they are different. They are disruptive. iTunes was created to sell single songs in order to stop piracy because full-length albums were far too much for teenagers to afford. Airbnb drastically changed the hotel game by providing accommodations to the world in rural and urban areas. Hailing a cab is a thing of the past now that we have apps for Uber and Lyft. These are new systems, based on old systems, but they are not just functional improvements. They are new systems in general.

> *"Companies preach creativity, hire for conformity and call consultants when they fail who tell them to be more creative."*
>
> *- Richie Norton*
> *#RiskTakerEdu*

What about school? In most cases, we still attend a physical building, with separations for students based on age. Educators are assigned a room and a curriculum and spend ten months a year building relationships before passing the class onward. Imagine having an Uber for students to call a teacher? Tutoring apps do exist where students can log in, ask questions, and speak to real educators from their own homes. The key difference is our students need ownership over their learning. They need to be accountable. They must want to learn. In my experience, most students just want to be told what to do, because that's what they've been trained to do. As students move up through the grades, I have noticed their curiosities diminish.

I do not believe students do not want to learn. I do believe some systems are responsible for sucking the joy out of learning. I am guilty of quickly writing off kids as "lazy" when I would be naive to think our school system didn't help contribute to this. If I was asked to sit at my desk all day and push paper, I'd feel lazy too.

Grades are a major barrier to change. Grades are excuses for doing what we have always done. Grades are the reason we test kids with timed exams. Grades create fear. Grades create anxiety. Just last year I read about a principal being fired for helping a student cheat on a standardized test. The pressure this puts on educators and students does nothing to help improve learning.

So what do we do? Well, we innovate inside the box. We use our existing schools but change the moving parts internally. Perhaps we group kids based on interest rather than age. Many of us would argue that grouping kids based on an ability is a solution but I would argue that "ability" is too broad of a generalization to describe a student's hobbies and interests. Do they really lack ability in everything they do?

With technology, we can bring the world to our schools. We can bring our schools to the world. We can use augmented reality and virtual reality to take field trips. We can create dungeons and castles in Minecraft while studying medieval times.

> *Play is often talked about as if it were a relief from serious learning. But for children play is serious learning. Play is really the work of childhood.*
>
> - Mr. Rogers
> #RiskTakerEdu

What I appreciate about the use of technology is the sandbox learning environment it brings. Worksheets do nothing for differentiation. Sure, we can ask fewer questions and call it scaffolding but that is so contradictory to anything being considered standard. When we use tools like Scratch, Minecraft, FlipGrid or green screen, we let students play and immerse themselves in the learning. While we are looking for a student product to assess, our kids are learning a great deal more as a byproduct to the process. Like me in high school. I learned HTML to make a digital poster for Mrs. Boudreau. Pile on the soft skills. Grit. Rigour. Perseverance. Initiative. Our kids will demonstrate these skills while tinkering with new tools. You never want to get in an Uber where the driver learned to drive from worksheets.

"I need a math mark!"

How many times have you said this? How many times have you heard this? Maybe not math, but you get the idea. I've said it dozens, if not hundreds, of times in the last decade and a half. Must be report card reason, huh? My concern with this statement is that there exists an unwritten rule in which we are to fill mark books to accurately complete report cards.

Wrong.

We don't judge Sidney Crosby's ability to play hockey by the results of just one period. So that math mark you are looking for in a pinch? Not likely going to be an accurate representation of student learning. For far too long, time has been the constant at school. I want education to be that constant, making time the changing variable.

The beauty of technology is that time no longer has to be a constant. That seventy-five minute math period, although structured by a physical location for attendance reasons, can occur outside the school day. Why do we all have to be in the same location at the same time? I work better in the morning than in the evening but that isn't the case for all of us. Posting work, videos, ideas, reflections, and assignments online allows students an opportunity to learn on their own. I trust my students to learn the material and be ready to challenge me on it. If I notice a student acting out, I'll call them out. But I also trust that they will get their work done before I see them the next day.

"I need a math mark!"

This statement implies immediacy. Quick and easy. I have a forty-minute period to hammer this out. Let's do a quiz. Been there, done that. At the end of the day, my professional judgment about student learning matched the results of that quiz. I created stress and anxiety, for me and them, for nothing. Nothing. But I felt better having that tangible, concrete evidence. This is a mindset we must shift.

Student artifacts are what we typically use for assessment and evaluation but we should also consider observations and conversations. Anecdotal evidence carries more weight than any test or exam I have given. Using my camera app, I can take pictures all year long of students engaged in their learning. I can send these pictures to them and have them record an audio overlay explaining what they are doing. We can create digital portfolios that demonstrate growth over the entire year, something the end of the year exam won't even demonstrate.

The notion of time can be significantly detrimental to student learning. When I was a student, our class was split into teams and we had to crunch multiplication facts correctly and faster than other teams to win the game. Let me pause for a second. Multiplication facts, like any other foundational learning, are vital. It is necessary to solve higher-order thinking problems. Receiving a C- on a test because you ran out of time might be a time management issue, not a lack of knowledge. When we were placed in our teams and faced against opposing players, how quickly you could spout correct answers made you a *good* math student. The faster you were, the better you were. Well, I was never really fast. I used my fingers to count and needed a few seconds just to process the question being thrown at me. Did this make me dumb? Of course not. The only reason we time student activities is because of that bell. Ditch the bell. Let kids eat when they are hungry. Take learning breaks as necessary. Disrupt the daily schedule. We teach our kindergarten students to listen to their bodies. Are you tired? Are you hungry? Grab a snack. Then suddenly in first-grade, the bell dictates when students can eat.

Ironically, students who need more time are given an IEP, a legal document stating the requirements for student learning. Imagine if all kids had one? How cool would that be? This doesn't mean more work for us. Heck, I'd argue it means less. On a side note, we really need to stop judging an entire class by how many IEPs it has. These are people, not documents.

Back to all students having their own learning plan. Technology created time for me in my classroom. I had my preps back! How many prep periods have you used to create pages, photocopy pages, and staple pages? How many preps have you spent just trying to figure out who handed in their assignments so you can go chasing those who did not from other classrooms? Technology solves these problems. In fact, my last year in the classroom, I was showing up later in the morning and leaving at the bell at the end of the day! Disrupt the schedule! Using Google Classroom, I no longer had to chase kids. I could email them, and their parents. I could use Google Forms if I needed to ask questions or have students reflect. By the way, I have no affiliation with Google, just that my former school board used it.

Take my word for it. The more access to technology we can provide, the richer the learning experience becomes for all. So naturally differentiated and scaffolded that when kids create content, they do so to the best of their ability. You know that student with an IEP who needs accommodations? I used to ask that student fewer questions as per that document.

"Find the volume of these three pyramids (as opposed to eight)."

Boooooring.

Instead, I might prompt with:

"How many different shaped pools can you make in Minecraft that have a specific volume?"

Same question, but worded but differently. The second prompt will make this child think. Rather than telling him or her to do fewer questions, and make them feel dumb about it, they have the freedom to try their best. Build success. Feel confident. Sure there might be eight different pool shapes and the student only made three, but, to me, this is a huge win. When students feel confident, they will take greater risks. Same holds true for staff.

The Kids Are Alright!
By Debra Hake (@MsHake418)

I was assaulted by a student this year. Twenty-two years in the classroom, and I never thought it would happen to me, but it did. Though it is an event that is in the realm of possibility when teaching secondary level education, even writing the words now it seems surreal. Yet, that is not what this blog is about. I want to focus on what students did right. What students do right on a daily basis. Most importantly, despite being attacked, what brought me back and why I'm staying.

It was the day before Halloween when it happened. What began as a routine cell phone confiscation landed me flat on my back, befuddled. I am a petite person, five foot two inches on a day I'm feeling especially confident. The student who assaulted me was an athlete and strong; my little body flew. My head bounced against the tile floor before my body finally landed several feet from where the incident occurred. I suffered a concussion, a lot of bruising, a stiff neck and my back will never be the same.

For the one student who exercised poor judgement that particular day in October, another 35 chose to act differently. As my assailant grabbed his phone and hit the door running, two students were on the phone to the office for emergency assistance. While two more students attended to me on the ground, one used their own jacket to prop up my head. The emergency training they had endured twice a year since Kindergarten was put into action like a well rehearsed performance.

It was scary. I already suffer from moderate anxiety as well, and it took me a few months of physical as well as emotional recovery before I could entertain the idea of returning. Short term memory loss plagued me, as well as sleeplessness. I could only take short trips from home. Mundane activities such as going to the grocery store were difficult, and I would only go during quiet hours.

The idea of a career change did cross my mind. If I could not go grocery shopping, how could I face the class where I had been assaulted? Self-doubt as an educator was ever present.

"Where had I gone wrong?" filled my thought process more times than I can relay. Yet, I underestimated the one part of this job which keeps us coming back as educators - the students.

I received cards, emails, gifts, flowers and even stuffed animals from them. Staff and families sent well wishes. How could someone not feel the love? By January, there was nothing that would keep me from my classroom, yet, I won't lie, it wasn't easy.

I've had people, mostly outside of education, ask me how I could return? It is unfathomable to most, but teachers, they get it. There is only one reason, the kids. I could focus on the one student who assaulted me back in October, but instead I chose to focus on the many amazing students who did the right thing and who continue to do the right thing every day.

My classroom is my second home; it has been my single constant for over two decades and the thought of never returning wasn't an option for this teacher. Teaching is in my blood, and every thought process I have. How could I not return?

I came back second semester, and yet I knew there were students in my class who had taken the side of my assailant. They were friends, and there was nothing I could do about it. I'm here to teach the students in my class on any given day, and I can not choose who they are; hence the journey began.

I won't lie, the anxiety was a mighty force at first. Every day at lunch time, before the class started, my heart would beat faster, I'd get headaches, and my hands would tremble.

After all these years in the classroom, I felt like a new teacher again, and I knew it was not going to be an easy process, but I made myself. I have had people tell me how brave I am for returning, yet for me, I needed to get over the fear of being in my own classroom. I need to reconnect with the students who had reached out, and focus on those students who did want to learn.

Slowly, day by day, the assault became a distant memory for my students and myself. The same class I was assaulted and having panic attacks in has become one of my favorite classes today. Working past the assault, my classroom is now a world of innovation. It is controlled chaos, an explorer's paradise and a place where risk is welcome and fostered. We are constantly in motion, in dialogue and creating. What looks like bedlam to some, is a symphony of learning to me.

Today, those same students like coming to my class. I say that because my biggest critics in October are the ones who tell me how much they like coming now that it is May. We've done more projects, experimental lessons, investigational exercises and technology than I ever have in the past. It makes for an exciting synergy in the room which I adore walking into on a daily basis.

As I reflect on the year, it seems only appropriate the class which gave me the most anxiety, is also the class which produced the most reward. It bothers me when adults complain about "kids these days." The kids I see on a daily basis are tenacious, polite and globally minded. In my book, the kids are alright.

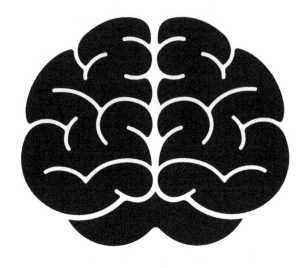

MINDSET

"Mind is a flexible mirror, adjust it, to see a better world."

- Amit Ray
#RiskTakerEdu

Previously I wrote about no longer having my own classroom. Three years ago I went back to grad school and completed my Master of Professional Education in Mathematics. Fancy schmancy title, eh? This was not an easy task for me. I mentioned before that my undergraduate degree is in Computer Science. When I enrolled I thought it would be the perfect fit. It ended up being the perfect fit, but let me elaborate on the blip I experienced early on.

First, academic writing is important and should be a part of academia. Or should it? Is this one of those "we've always done it this way" cases? I don't even know anymore. Long story short, I bombed my very first paper I wrote because my APA style was atrocious. Well, of course, I was a CS major now looking to study math learning. If my memory serves me, something like twenty percent of my mark was style, implying *how* I wrote was as important as *what* I wrote. This hit me hard. For the first time, I felt like that third-grade kid struggling to complete a standardized test. Like me, he didn't know the rules. He didn't know he couldn't write outside the box. If he did, he was deducted points. Is there fairness in this type of assessment? Not sameness, but fairness?

So there I was, first year of a two year Master's program and losing my mind during the first course because I did not know how to write an APA style paper. I knew it was going to be a long, winding road.

I wasn't sure I could even do it. Alas, I did some Googling, did some Khan Academy and YouTube watching and managed to do slightly better during the next assignment. Frustrated, I finally reached out to the prof and asked if I could create content for the internet instead of burying my ideas in a PDF online journal. He obliged and the Hour of Curiosity was born (www.hourofcuriosity.com). I spent the next two years curating research, archiving documents and creating coding tutorials for math integration. The site is still live today.

Finishing grad school was a massive accomplishment. One of my most memorable and cherished moments second to winning the Canadian Prime Minister's Award for Teaching Excellence in 2016. Finishing grad school meant I could now teach at the university level, which is where I still remain at the time of this book. I now teach teachers at a variety of Faculties of Education here in Ontario. This has taught me a great deal about our school system.

In Ontario, a teacher's salary is based on two factors: level of education and experience. It takes ten years for a teacher to max their experience salary but their level of education can change anytime they wish to take more courses. Our Additional Qualification courses are made up of three parts - Part 1, Part 2 and Part 3, the Specialist course. Obtaining a specialist means all three parts have been completed.

Educators who wish to pursue administration require a minimum of two specialists, or six courses, before they can register for a principal's qualification. OK, I know. Why am I telling you?

I am very fortunate to teach all three sections of IICT (Integration of Information and Computer Technology) as well as a math course. It is incredibly inspiring to instruct teachers from across my great province and see what their school boards are up to as they also provide ways to integrate coding and computational thinking into their lessons. However, your level of experience dictates which section you may enroll in.

Educators fresh out of school can enroll in any Part One section of any course. Educators need two years minimum teaching to take a Part Two section and five years teaching the subject area to qualify to enroll in the Specialist.

Why am I telling you this?

Well. The mindset among educators in all three sections is vastly different. I have noticed those enrolled in my Part One sections are very grade heavy. They want marks and they talk about all the marking they do in their classrooms. However, those enrolled in my Part Three sections, having five years minimum experience, and potentially pursuing a leadership position, could care less about what they got as a mark. They want feedback. They want feedback from me. They want feedback from their peers. Remember, these are more veteran teachers who have expanded their pedagogies. In no way am I criticizing those educators taking Part One. I am simply pointing out a correlation. These are the people who have just left university. That place where grades matter most. And so the cycle begins again. We need grades to get into university. Do you recognize the pattern and see the problem? The more and more educators gain experience, the more the focus becomes on giving great feedback and less on testing and grades. The educators in my Part One sections don't have any experience. Many are supply teachers. They only know how they have been taught.

I feel a major disconnect. When we recognize all students as being unique, why are Faculties of Education focusing so much emphasis on standardization? How many times have you taken on a student teacher and encouraged them to forget their university experience at the Faculty because it is about to get real in the trenches? And those Teacher's Guides you read? They are not written for your typical classroom. They seem to be written for this false sense of reality where all kids come to school, after eating a great breakfast, engaged, prepared and ready to learn. I especially love the prompts that suggest the Teacher's Guide knows how my students will respond. Priceless.

Ditch the script. The more formal the lesson plan I wrote, the more frustrated I would get when we didn't follow it precisely. Frustration lead to me losing my temper, which often lead to punishment. Not discipline, but punishment. Remember, there is a difference. And remember it is OK to be where you are, it is not OK to stay there.

In a nutshell, our universities are doing a great job of training adults, new teachers, that what mark they received outweighs what they have learned. Grade-focused. Super-competitive before even jumping on a supply teacher list! We need to fix this.

Disruption
By Chris Woods (@DailyStem)

Disrupting is such a powerful word. I suppose "disrupting" is the opposite of "rupting," but I don't know what rupting is. Maybe it's like fake lava "erupting" from a science fair volcano, but that's kind of what I want my classroom to be. Exciting, filled with risk, and a little messy.

I do know that when we create a culture of disrupting in education, we're deciding to "be the change" we want to see in education. We're not settling for a classroom like the one we grew up in, because that world doesn't exist anymore. We're choosing instead to make our classroom a place filled with authentic learning experiences, not contrived story problems or meaningless worksheets. And we're choosing to leave the sidelines (or teacher's lounge) and share the successes and failures from our classroom with other teachers. And disrupters like us are hard at work everywhere, sharing our stories and ideas in books and podcasts. We're not sitting in the teacher's lounge complaining about problems, we're sharing our solutions and successes on social media and at conferences.

I decided to be a disrupter in education and started sharing the ideas from my classroom to help change the STEM mindset. Because I know that when most people hear the term STEM, they immediately think about robots and 3-D printing and expensive kits and fancy labs. And I do agree, that's part of STEM, like the part that shows up on school newsletters and local interest stories on the TV news. But in my classroom, disrupting takes a different form. I show my students ways that STEM intersects with their lives on a daily basis, and I try to make it as simple and relevant and inexpensive as possible.

Have you ever seen a video on YouTube that made you think "I wonder how they did that?" or "that was really amazing?" Those are the videos I show my students every day. They love seeing things that people are making or interesting jobs that people have or funny inventions that people make. And most of those have some STEM connections while only taking up 1 to 5 minutes of class time.

These kinds of videos are perfect to play at the start of class to engage discussion or in the middle of class to perk up students who have started to daydream. Or better yet, show them the end of class to leave students with something to contemplate until tomorrow's class.

I'm also guessing you have a phone in your pocket. That's good. The next time you see a road sign that's a polygon, or a package of paper towels that says six rolls is equal to nine rolls, pull it out and take a picture. Those photos become real starting points for a lesson or the basis of relevant story problems (because we all know kids love to ask "When are we ever gonna use this anyway?") My phone (and Twitter) is filled with pictures and videos I can use to get kids discussing and thinking about various STEM topics. And now when I walk through the lunchroom, kids show me their rectangle shaped pizza and triangle shaped quesadillas and ask me to "take a picture of this STEM I found."

Do you hand out worksheets in your class? Do the kids complete them and then forget what they've learned? I'm not always happy just giving a worksheet. I want kids to understand "why" math problems work, not just "how" they work. So I frequently hand out paper and scissors and tape ("Mr Woods, we're not 3rd graders!") and we start cutting and creating. Maybe I ask them to "cut out pieces that would make a triangular prism" and challenge them to use the most surface area possible. When kids manipulate something in their hands, when they make it themselves, they understand it better and value the learning.

Oh, and I'm done giving my students projects in my classroom. They've come to expect "projects" as something to be completed, something to be handed in, something that just gets them an A or a C or an F. I now call them "challenges," an open-ended opportunity to see a problem, try a solution, and keep improving on their iterations, much like they'll experience at their job someday. Do they still get "credit" for doing it? Sure, but the score is no longer the motivation. Learning and creating something amazing have become the new goal.

Do we tell kids to read every day? Of course we do. In the same breath we should also be telling them to do some STEM every day. That's the only way that STEM will leave it's "silo" (yes, it's already been built) and become part of their every day life. What I really desire is for kids to see STEM as something that relates to everything that they're passionate about. Whether that's horses or music or sports or movies or video games, there's STEM there waiting to be discovered.

I want politicians to see that STEM is not just a talking point or something to allocate funds for, but something that helps kids practice valuable skills like creating and innovating and working together. I want teachers to see STEM as the application of their content standards or subject area, something that intersects with reading and writing and history and art and culture. I want parents to see STEM as more than rocket science, something that they can easily do with their kids in the kitchen, garage, or backyard. In our classrooms and schools and homes, we need to help kids see that what they learn matters. If you just want to keep teaching kids how to be successful in school, go ahead. I'll be busy helping kids get ready for the world!

NETWORKING

> *"Talent wins games, but teamwork and intelligence win championships."*
>
> *- Michael Jordan*
> *#RiskTakerEdu*

The population of the planet has more than doubled in the last fifty years. At seven and a half billion, surely there is someone for everybody. We also have close to fifty billion devices connected to the internet. That is about seven devices per person, if my math is correct. This will bring a massive disruption to the education space.

We can no longer ban devices. We can no longer use devices as a reward system. Devices can no longer be used as an event but rather embedded in practice and used to enhance the learning experience. There is no such thing as "off and away" any longer. Buckle up for the big data era. The second biggest disruption education has seen following the internet and social media.

You know how you call tell it is Data Management season in elementary schools? You have a plethora of kids walking the halls carrying clipboards, interrupting other classes to ask surveys.

Knock Knock.

"Hello?"
"Can we ask your class a survey?"
"Well of course! We can finish our lesson afterwards."

"What is your favorite color?"

"What is your favorite pizza topping?"
"What is your favorite video game?"

I've done this. You have too, don't deny it. But what were we collecting this data for? Because our curriculum says so, that's why. Well, who cares. Sorry, not me. This data serves no real purpose to me. And there are a gazillion ways to collect authentic data.

I stopped asking students to scour the school for survey responses immediately when Google Forms dropped. Finally, a tool that could do most of that strand of math.

Data Management:
- Collect, organize and display data
- Make predictions
- Make assumptions
- Graph data using multiple sources

Yep. Google Forms can do all that. But that doesn't mean we still shouldn't collect data. Let me share with you one of my most popular tweets this calendar year, which was tweeted on June 6, 2019.

I am teaching a University course - Teaching and Learning Through eLearning. Many teacher participants are new to Twitter. I am trying to demonstrate the power of the #PLN.

Can you reply here and tell us where you are tweeting from this morning and what it is you do or teach?

The idea was simple. I was trying to demonstrate the power of social media for the educators in my courses as well as show how social media can be used to gather data. If you are not on Twitter, now is the time to do so! My followers can see most of this data too. With the exception of the specific tweet analytics, the general public has access to the number of replies, likes and retweets this tweet has garnered. Let us dissect this a bit further. At the time of this writing:

Impressions: 193,992
Profile clicks: 1,291
Replies: 1,128
Detail expands: 874
Likes: 630
Hashtag clicks: 432
Retweets: 66
Follows: 4
Link clicks: 1

This single tweet was been seen almost two hundred thousand times in only three weeks! This is data I want to know about! As a class, we could make a hashtag since mine in this example was clicked over four hundred times. Imagine following your hashtag stats during a semester. But perhaps, the most significant data point is the number of replies. Over a thousand people took the time to reply to me. I wonder how much time that took, assuming the average tweet takes a few dozen seconds? A great inquiry question! If I were a Geography teacher, I just landed on a pot of gold. Over a thousand locations we can now explore using Street View. Over a thousand locations we can make inferences about. Over a thousand locations we can tour and learn about and make connections to students there too. This is powerful stuff! We could extend this idea by exploring stats based on time of day. I live in the Eastern Time zone so I am strategic about the time of day I tweet. I wonder if this tweet would be more or less successful if I tweeted it in the morning versus the evening? So much to ponder. So much to wonder! Now I am curious!

A simple example, but a powerful one. While collecting data, you are connecting with other classrooms. Imagine the possibilities! Mystery Skype, Google Hangouts, pen pals? The list is practically infinite.

"What you have to do and the way you have to do it is incredibly simple. Whether you are willing to do it is another matter."

- Peter Drucker
#RiskTakerEdu

Being mindful of the big data era will be crucial in our schools. From now on, every decision we make is tracked. Every behaviour we display is marketed. Every word we speak to Alexa is saved. Data. Big data. And our kids need to know about this. I'll use this opportunity to promote my first book, Code Breaker. Get kids coding so they at least know how these machines work! And so you at least know how these machines work too!

Collecting data doesn't just have to be on social media. I love having students create apps and games with Scratch, Makey Makey, and Micro:Bit to also collect data. It could be the speed of a Sprite, the score of a game or even just the odds of winning Rock, Paper, Scissors. The beauty here lies in the fact that math was used to create content in other subject areas. Maybe the game is about habitats? Maybe the game is about making words like Boggle? Coding is a fantastic way to spiral curriculum and explore multiple expectations from across content areas with one project. Once their projects are complete, I usually share them on my Instagram Story because that is a common place kids hang out these days. When I share student work on my Instagram Story, students ask to be tagged. Remember, I DO friend them on social media. After all, why not?

What makes Instagram Story special is that students take the virtual tour of their work home and show their parents, who quite often, also follow me on Instagram. It is imperative to be connected. Educators who live in isolation have chosen to do so. Carve your digital footprint and teach students to do the same. And of course, Instagram Story also has metrics, so back to that Data Management and Geography lesson!

Bring Your Appetite For Disruption!
By Jeff Kubiak (@jeffreykubiak)

According to our friends at Websters and Oxford, the word "disruption" has several meanings; my favorite being "An interruption in the process".

As educators, we hear this word being used almost as frequently as "differentiation", or "21st Century". But what is it that we are really doing when we have a thirst or appetite for "Disruption"?

Breaking the mold, doing something very unconventional, and even unpopular. If we are to truly hit the mark in the future with our students in mind, then we must be constantly iterating, and improving upon practices, methods or styles that may work, have worked, or perhaps have failed.

With students on the forefront of our cerebral cortex at all times, it is especially effective to truly tune in and watch these amazing critters work and tick. What are they doing? What really drives them? How can I better partner with this child and really light a torch?

If we aren't asking ourselves these questions throughout the day and week, then the undeniable truth of change has passed us by once again.

In the world of education, students are our domain. Our drive. Our work, and our passion (at least they should be). Look at some examples of what I'd call disruption that have made strides in student driven facilitation - or good teaching…

- Flexible Seating (yes, another buzzword) - when the first few teachers or students began to say "Hey, why do we all have to sit on these prison made chairs?" Instead, someone looked at what might be comfortable, mobile, adjustable, friendly and malleable to make the environment of a classroom/school realistic to the actual needs of our movin' and groovin' kids!

- Alternative modelled schools - to name a few; AltSchool, Khan Lab, High Tech High, Innova Schools, and XP School. What they've done is focused on the what ifs, why nots and let's try, instead of the past and then. These places are NUTS! The way the campus' are laid out, eating areas, teaching style and pedagogy, play facilities...the list goes on and on and why? Because it is what our students need!

So here's my challenge to you, me and all of us. Keep that thirst. Listen to your hunger and let your imagination run wild. We have an obligation to serve our students tomorrow's needs, today. What that means is this; get whacky, try stuff, be crazy (but safe) and find something mind-blowing. Oh, yeah. You may just want to ask a group of students what they want or need too, I heard we are working FOR them.

TENACITY

"Many of life's failures are people who did not realize how close they were to success when they gave up."

- Thomas A. Edison
#RiskTakerEdu

Have you ever heard the story of WD40? You know that oil spray found in most homes? It was always my go-to as a kid when needing to grease up that rusty bicycle chain. WD40. But what does that stand for? This is a story of perseverance. Of tenacity. Of trial and error. Of risk-taking. Of learning from failure. Beginning in 1953, the company set out to create a line of degreasers and rust prevention solvents but just couldn't seem to manage the right formula. Until their fortieth attempt!

Imagine that. Forty tries. Thirty-nine failures. Or were they? How we perceive and define failure says a lot about our teaching philosophies. Rarely do students get a do-over after an exam period. But when working on projects, they have the freedom to fail. Freedom to explore. Freedom to learn.

WD40. The fortieth formula worked! Water Displacement, the fortieth formula. That's the name straight from the lab book used by the chemist who started the product. Amazing!

Back at the school level, we typically assign grades at the end of a unit, regardless of the fact that the curriculum states that these are end of the year goals. How often do we give students a second chance? How often do we give students a third chance? Here is the kicker. Giving chances doesn't change a thing without proper feedback. I surely never want to try and try again without making any changes created by the guidance of a professional. Didn't Einstein define *insanity* as doing the same over and over but expecting different results? Imagine giving students thirty-nine chances to get something right. I could get behind this but it would require a massive overhaul of some of our current logistics. Time. Bells. Minutes. Structures. Policies. You get it. It is easier for our elementary friends who get to spend most days with students whereas our secondary counterparts typically get one period a day. Stories like WD40 are not as rare as one might think.

Alas, sometimes we get things right the first time. How many songs do you know that were written and recorded in one take? I could name a few. But I won't. Why? Great question. Because we never learn anything from being perfect. Learning happens when things don't go well. Learning happens when we are given an opportunity to reflect. To grow. To think. Learning happens when we focus our energy into a project that influences change and has a great deal of obstacles along the way.

> *When nothing is sure, everything is possible.*
>
> #RiskTakerEdu

I believe our future industry will be made up of freelance workers. That is, everyone will have a skill they can market and sell. Companies already outsource major portions of their day to day routines. Remember, the jobs of tomorrow don't exist yet and the problems our students will face have yet to be recognized. Truth is, we do not really know what is to come. That is why we call it the future.

Back to The Future was a major part of my youth. I loved all three movies and watched them on the regular. It was fun to actually wake up on October 21, 2015, the day and year Marty McFly and Doc Brown visit the future. Blows my mind that this is now my past.

I was teaching seventh- and eighth-grade in 2015. I remember celebrating Back to The Future Day with a movie marathon as well as many other lessons and activities in our Language Arts classes. As a class, we made predictions about what our futures would look like. Boy are our kids imaginative. Boy are our students creative. They live in a digital world far from my wheelhouse and as a result, typically make better predictions about technology.

So what does our future industry look like? I'm not entirely sure, but I do know that students will need a personal brand. They will all be Googled. Students need online portfolios showcasing their strengths.

Students need positive digital footprints and people who can blaze the trail for them. Role models who put themselves out there, online for the world to see. Make some noise. Be loud. Share far and wide and share often.

I've seen many "21st-century teacher" memes over the years and most do get it right. But simply having a podcast doesn't change much, unless it is used to influence change in others. In fact, I do not have a podcast. I do have a blog, however, and I use it to amplify other teachers' voices, much like I have done with this book. Why? Because we are all in this together. We are better together. Squad goals. Change is made when the masses generate a movement.

So what can you do in your classroom tomorrow? Well, many things. Start small. Choose one thing and do it well. Join Twitter and network with others. Write a blog. Create a classroom website. Just be sure not to get caught up in the buzz of social media. Sure, FlipGrid is an awesome tool, but only if you utilize it properly. I believe all kids can achieve if given a fair chance and that chance requires proper implementation of technology.

As I wrote in *Code Breaker*, the problems our students will face in life will not be solved by an app. But the way they learn to problem solve while using emerging technologies can help them develop solutions. What I love about this line is the idea of developing solutions. Not just finding answers, but developing authentic solutions to authentic problems.

The Beginner's Guide to Disrupting
By Andrew Arevalo (@Gameboydrew)

I hate to break it to you, but disruption isn't what you think it is. In fact, it's one of the most overused and misrepresented words in education. Adding to the complexity of this pervasive travesty is the fact that it's consistently hurled around by those with amplified megaphones that unequivocally lack the empathy to truly understand what it means and how it feels. We've gotten to the point where it's so watered down other terms now elicit a greater fight-or-flight emotional response. Don't believe me? Teach in the most conservative way possible. See what I mean?

For many though, disruption isn't just a "bang" word in a keynote. It's a life-altering choice and a means to an entirely different way of thinking, doing, and LIVING.

Before I share my story, let me tell you what disruption is. I don't mean to state the seemingly obvious, but I believe it's warranted - now more than ever. Disruption doesn't mean doing the same thing that everyone around you is doing. It means doing something so profoundly unique that all your beliefs and values are questioned in the process. It means going against the social constructs that have historically defined your place and prevented mobility because of your identity. It means building a ladder, climbing it, and then inviting those below you to climb above with you. It means being so disenfranchised with your reality that your only solution is to create a new one.

My mom and dad both worked long hours in the labor-intensive fields to put themselves through college and eventually became first-generation graduates.

What compelled their erratic behavior to pursue something so drastically different? Simple, grit and passion. And the fact that they couldn't buy-in to a life that didn't make sense or bring them happiness. By the way, that's real disruption for you!

I remember the first time I got accepted to speak at a national conference. The emotions I felt were both exhilarating and numbing. And for good reasons. I'm a 29-year-old Hispanic male educator from a small border community that most will never hear of. To put it nicely, these types of opportunities don't exist for individuals that come from El Centro. Unfortunately, my celebration quickly turned into utter despair and complete frustration. Per my district contract, traveling out-of-state to present wasn't permitted. In fact, if I wanted to go and share my ideas - I'd be docked a day's pay.

Have you ever been put into a situation where you felt compelled to do something you've never done before without any support and tangible quantitative consequences to bear with? I have, and fortunately my resolve wasn't swayed because I was grounded in my why. See, speaking in front of others was and always will be my what. Hence, I knew exactly why I needed to attend. I didn't make the decision lightly. At the time, I'd never even been out-of-state. In addition, don't forget, my livelihood (and mortgage payment) was dependent upon my salary. There was no monetary incentive for me to go - just an opportunity to inspire others to be better for kids. After looking back, did I make the right choice?

I'd like to think so, especially considering the fact that I just won a national teaching award, landed my first featured speaking gig, and have become a catalyst for others with similar backgrounds and stories.

In education, there are two types of people. Those that talk about disrupting the "status quo" . . . and those that don't have the time to talk because they are too busy shattering ceilings, establishing a legacy, and creating lasting ripples that future generations will forever feel. It's safe to say that Brian is a true rule breaker, and I'm happy to follow his lead. More than that, I'm humbled and beyond ecstatic that the notorious "Airport Selfie Guy" took a risk and gave me, Gameboydrew, an outlet to share a snippet of my story. With that being said, remember, the actions you take today can represent a bridge or an anchor for those that come after. Are you ready to take some risks?

COURAGE

"Being deeply loved by someone gives you strength, while loving someone deeply gives you courage."

- Lao Tzu
#RiskTakerEdu

A former principal of mine made a bold move one year when he decided we were all going to try operating a paperless classroom. The plan was two-fold; our school board at the time had just implemented a 1:1 program with iPads and our printing budget was through the roof.

Remember the days when you were given a stack of paper for the year and told that's all you get? Remember having to purchase more on your own if you wanted to print? Remember searching the printer drawers hoping someone had accidentally left their stash? Like searching for quarters in telephone booths we would scavenge the teacher's lounge hoping for a miracle. And boy, if you landed on that fancy expensive yellow or red paper, you had struck gold! An underground market of paper trading and paper stealing was in full force and we even had our students involved in some of the scheming.

Our printing budget that final year was something like twelve thousand dollars for a school of four hundred students. The plan was simple, I was given additional non-teaching time to help digitize our worlds. I was scanning textbooks, editing PDFs, dropping people in the Google Classroom world. There wasn't much pushback as no one was asked to change anything other than to try digitizing everything they do. SAMR was huge then and a simple substitution made sense.

SAMR (Substitution, Augmentation, Modification, Redefinition) is a model popularized by Dr. Ruben Puentedura that is designed to help teachers integrate technology into teaching and learning. The ultimate goal of SAMR is to transform learning experiences so they yield higher achievements.

I am incredibly proud of the work we did that year. It was a bold step for many, and 1:1 iPads was intimidating. Charging them. Syncing them. Monitoring them. Installing apps on them. This all required a massive shift in planning and thinking and our staff was very courageous in pulling it all together.

As an ironic and helpful byproduct of this process, we all began to change our pedagogy.

"My activity sheet is no good anymore because the kids are Googling the answers!"

I will never forget this statement made by a colleague. It wasn't said with a negative context but rather an "ah-ha" moment where she felt the iPad could do more. After all, she was given one too and was happily exploring this new device looking for augmented reality apps for Science class.

So, what began as a simple way to reduce printing costs became a massive cohort of educators looking to redefine their classroom activities. Digitizing paper content showed us that it might be time for an overhaul. No one complained and our students were enthralled with this new approach. Immediately we were green screening, coding, making, creating, sharing and collaborating in ways we never thought possible.

We went from quiet rows to exercise bikes and bouncy balls as seats all because we changed the way we thought about school.

And we reduced our printing budget to about three thousand by year three. We had saved almost twenty thousand dollars over three years and, in turn, bought more devices with that money. Where paper copies are single-use, iPads gave us years of opportunity.

Printing costs aside. iPads aside. Two new mottos were developed in those years. One I have written about previously in Block Breaker:

"It is OK to be where you are. It is NOT OK to stay there."

This rule applied to anyone who entered our building. Staff, students, parents, teachers, principals, custodians. Everyone.

The second motto, coined by our wicked awesome French teacher, was:

"Uncomfortable is the new norm. We have to be comfortable with discomfort."

Now that is courageous. Ba-bye status quo.

When I reflect back on this experience (which is almost a decade ago now!), I smile when remembering how colleagues challenged me and made me think. Perspective is everything and where I might have excelled with technology, others excelled with experience and imagination.

Perhaps it's a more common task now, but I will never forget watching a veteran colleague in her last few years of teaching, creating a green screen on the floor so that her Sphero could act as the Mars Rover since the class was studying space.

Mind. Blown.

A green screen on the floor? What will she think of next?!?!

It was incredibly innovative at the time and lead us to other unconditional ideas like putting Lego on the wall and building arcades at school!

Now that we had iPads, we could document our learning in new, innovative ways! I built my first stand up arcade that year with the help of my students and that wicked awesome French teacher I mentioned earlier. There are still some YouTube videos on my channel showing us painting, sanding, priming and playing Teenage Mutant Ninja Turtles. Not only were our students playing games, they were coding them too. There was a tremendous amount of curriculum involved and the iPad captured every moment.

Sure, we had electronic parts in a wooden box and a soldering iron heating up to connect wires. Perhaps not quite up to health and safety standards but I'm willing to bet those kids will never forget it. Of course, safety was our top priority, and some rules had to be bent to accomplish our goals.

I have very fond memories of that school. I met a ton of amazing people who I admire and respect and continue to learn from to this day. Yes, I am writing this in past tense as much has changed since then. But to think, what began as a simple way to reduce printing costs allowed us to blaze a new trail for those students as well as ourselves. Colleagues, who after thirty years of teaching, were determined to finish their careers with a paperless classroom full of STEM, STEAM and robotic activities.

Now that is courageous.

Regrets of a First year Teacher
By Brian Aspinall

Originally posted: January 6, 2016 on brianaspinall.com

I must make a confession as this has been bothering me for quite some time. It has been a reoccurring thought on my morning commute to school over the last few months. When I landed my first teaching job I was ecstatic. It was a grade 5 position, and I was the third "constant" teacher to enter the classroom that year for a variety of reasons. The environment was somewhat chaotic due to a lack of consistently and I was determined to do my best.

But I made a really bad choice.

I quickly learned there existed a rotating computer schedule in this classroom. There were two desktop computers at the back of the class and students had scheduled opportunities to sit and work or play at these machines when the schedule said it was their turn, even during class time. I remember trying to teach a lesson when two students got up, headed over to the computers and began playing. As you can imagine, I was in shock. Such disrespect, or so I thought. Turns out this was how it worked – students would watch the clock until it was their turn, get up and tag each other out.

The next day I decided I was going to show them who was boss and I ripped up the schedule in front of the class. A great way to start the day. I made firm statements about new rules and routines and stressed the hierarchical structures. I was even complimented for getting them all to sit quietly so I thought I was doing the right thing.

Today, I am embarrassed to admit my actions for a variety of reasons.

I have no idea why the schedule existed in the first place, but I was the newbie to the class so I should have let them explain it. As much as it didn't make sense to me, it did to someone else. Perhaps the class made up the rule as a group – I will never know – but I should have asked questions and made new routines with their help, not because I didn't agree. After all, they were in grade 5 and this was March so the routine was very much embedded. I ruled with a iron fist and now wonder what it was like to be a grade 5 student in that class. Doesn't sound fun and goes against every pedagogical belief I have today.

However, I went to school in quiet hierarchical rows and I learned to teach at the Faculty in very similar settings. I was complimented for getting them to conform so I continued to dictate because I needed to impress the hiring committee. There existed a silo / fishbowl in that best practice was shared in the staffroom and I wasn't up to par based solely on the volume of my class.

I've come to realize that "classroom management" can take on a variety of definitions ranging from quiet, attentive students – to loud, empowered kids who react to your prompts immediately. I understand the textbook principles to classroom management but also acknowledge the one size fits all model does not suffice and nobody knows your students better than you.

So, to you twenty-somethings now, I apologize for taking away that schedule without asking questions. It's not as much about the deprivation of computer time as it is about asking the right questions, treating you like people and coming up with an improved solution that worked for everyone. I was focused on compliance – as the noise level dictated how well you "managed" a class and I needed a job. You only have one first impression, and I made mine. I'm not making excuses, just suggesting a justification for my actions. I was the outsider and it wasn't right for me to make assumptions and changes about your classroom without first getting to know you.

Thank you for listening, I feel a little better.

RISK

"Sometimes the greatest PD is the teacher down the hall."

#RiskTakerEdu

Every time I hit that publish button on a new blog post I feel incredibly vulnerable. The moment we decide to share ideas with the world, we open doors for feedback, critique, and criticism. As I decided early on in my career, sharing my ideas only makes me better, especially when engaging in positive discourse with others. Being transparent in our learning is vital for personal and professional growth.

However, feeling vulnerable includes having self-doubt, insecurities, and even anxiety, all of which often lead to other poor choices to avoid thinking this way. Maybe we binge-watch Netflix, have a few cocktails, or just find that bag of chips to comfort ourselves as we wait for the storm to pass. The truth is, our students quite often feel this way on a daily basis. We ask them to share thoughts in a public forum, surrounded by their peers all waiting for something to be said.

"Phew, she didn't pick me!"

I remember thinking this when I was a student.

I also remember thinking up ways to sound smart just in case I was her next shame victim. Shame and vulnerability go hand in hand.

We are all human and this is a part of what makes us human. But it is our integrity that determines how we channel this negative energy and how we model the approach to feeling vulnerable for our students.

Yesterday was the first day of school here in Ontario. Yes, that means I have been writing for two months. Some days I wake up excited to continue this project. Other days I worry what people will think, say, or even do. Who in their right mind wants to put themselves in that kind of situation?

But we must. We have to. We ask our students to do this daily.

Finding our insecurities better prepares us for future situations when we begin to recognize patterns. I have found the more I express this in front of students, the better I feel. The more I admit my own self-doubt and insecurities, the more confident I find my students. The more I admit my anxieties and stressors, the more my students engage with me as a person and recognize me as more than just their teacher.

Every time I hit that publish button on a new blog post, I pause, take a breath and remember why I do what I do. This is about me trying to leave my mark in hopes that I can make even one school day special for even just one student.

I encourage you to make a list of things that make you feel anxious. Maybe it is school, maybe it is colleagues. Maybe it is money or family life. Now ask your students to do the same. Invite them to a community circle where everyone can share what makes them want to crawl under a rock. This way, we can recognize and predict our own feelings, which allows us to better cope and find solutions. It is human nature to want to engage in avoidance techniques the moment we feel anxious. Just make it go away!

Taking risks means trying new things which requires us to be vulnerable. Playing it safe doesn't allow space for growth. You never learn anything from being perfect.

Once students have created a list of stressors, ask them to reflect and think about each one in a specific situation.

"I don't want to share in math class because I don't want to sound dumb."

How often do you speak up at staff meetings or professional development days? I've been known to quietly try to hide behind my phone for fear of ridicule from colleagues. Which is incredibly ironic because that would hardly ever happen. For the most part, my colleagues have all been incredibly supportive.

"I don't want to change for gym class because I don't want to be called fat."

How does body dysmorphia affect your bathing suit choices? I've been known to skip meals because I ate too much for lunch. On a daily basis, I am counting calories in my head, trying to determine that appropriate balance, which only makes me more anxious. I will jog and overextend myself physically as punishment for eating too much the night before. The continuous feeling of anxiety only makes me more anxious. This is the first time I have shared some of my own demons in a public forum and I am scared as hell about how you might perceive me. But here I am.

Break the cycle.

Be vulnerable.

Take the leap.

Every time I hit that publish button on a new blog post I feel inspired. Or at least, I am working on that. Just like I have made a list of stressors that make me anxious, I have also made a list of items that inspire me. I encourage you to do the same and I encourage you to ask your students to do the same.

When we can predict our own behaviour, we are in full control of it. Take what makes you anxious and transfer it to what inspires you.

The first time I spoke in front of a group of teachers I was a wreck. Shaking, sweating, stuttering. I was a mess. My wife was there too and she could tell. But I did it. I practiced ahead of time, made a beautiful slide deck and, as you would expect, had some pushback during my presentation.

Oh shit.

My nervousness lead to more sweating, which lead to more anxiety. A terrible cycle of mental hell with me wanting it to all go away as soon as possible. What a moron I am to think I have anything good to share!

But what came from this was a wonderful conversation and new-found friends. You see, it wasn't me that was being challenged but rather an idea of mine. There is a difference and this helps me find inspiration, not stress.

My presentation ended with a standing ovation. Not as much because of my content, but because of my honesty. That moment forever changed my teaching career. The energy and anxiety, coupled together, allowed me to be vulnerable, which allowed me to learn. I learned that sharing your ideas makes everyone better.

So speak up.

***

> *"Only those who will risk going too far can possibly find out how far it is possible to go."*
>
> *- T.S. Eliot*
> #RiskTakerEdu

This summer I took the biggest risk of my career. I resigned from my school board.

I have been on a Leave of Absence for three years while finishing grad school and teaching at various Faculties of Education here in Ontario, Canada.

Along this journey, I have met some amazing educators! What an opportunity I have been given. I teach teachers. I teach new teachers. I teach veteran teachers.

But I no longer have a pension.

I no longer have summers off.
I no longer have a regular paycheque.

However, with risk comes reward. For the last decade I have been pushing for more STEM / STEAM integration in schools and now I am very fortunate to be able to consult for various school districts across North America and continue the cause. Speaking at conferences is one of my most favorite things to do.

And I still feel anxious.

Every. Single. Time.

So why do I do it?

I feel that I have a responsibility to continue with my own Passion Project. I am simply practicing what I preach and I want to see it through. I want to expose as many students to Computer Science as possible. Why? Because you do not know if you like broccoli until you try it.

So here I am. Writing the last chapter of this book on the second day of school in September, of which I am no longer affiliated.

And Kawhi Leonard is no longer a Raptor.

"There are some really ambitious teachers out there trying to make change. Teachers like Brian Aspinall."

This was paraphrased to me this last weekend and this one simple statement put all of my fears, all of my stressors, and all of my insecurities into context.

This is why I took the risk.

This is why I am writing my vulnerabilities in this book.

It feels good to speak my truths. I can't possibly be alone in this thinking.

This is what makes taking risks so special. You won't find success with every risk you take, but if you were to graph the line of best fit over a lifetime, you would see an increase in positivity.

Never give up on being better. You might find things rough for a while, but this just makes for an opportunity to try something new. Face adversity head-on, be bold, be creative, be honest, be transparent, be vulnerable, and, most important, be you.

01010010 01101001 01110011 01101011

ABOUT THE AUTHOR

Brian Aspinall is an educator and best-selling author who is considered one of the brightest STEAM innovators in Canadian education. His books, *Code Breaker* and *Block Breaker* continue to top the charts in STEM education with a focus on rethinking assessment and evaluation. Recently he was awarded the Prime Minister's Award for Teaching Excellence for his work with coding and computational thinking. His enthusiasm, thought leadership, and approach to building capacity within STEAM education has made him a sought-after speaker throughout North America and has earned him the honour of being selected as Canada's first Minecraft, Micro:Bit, and Makey Makey Ambassador!

BRING BRIAN TO YOUR SCHOOL OR EVENT!

Twenty-first-century learning requires students to create, collaborate, and think critically. Progress "STEMs" directly from immediate feedback and a personalized learning platform. Coding forces students to problem-solve, make mistakes, and overcome barriers because programs can only run if written correctly. In this workshop, teachers will learn the basics of block-based coding and how to make use of mathematical principles to create content for learning.

In this workshop, participants will learn about the history and pedagogy of computer science, its importance for the future, and how to integrate it into existing curricula. With a focus on twenty-first-century competencies, participants will explore assessment and evaluation while engaging in the process of learning.

Brian is a former elementary teacher and current university instructor on a mission to expose as many kids as he can to coding and computer science. In his passionate talks, he makes a case for the importance of exposing youth to the principles of coding and computational thinking to prepare them for their rapidly changing future.

TEDX TALKS

Beyond Rote Learning (Chatham, ON)
Published March 14, 2014

Education Reform (Chatham, ON)
Published June 16, 2015

Hacking the Classroom (Kitchener, ON)
Published June 16, 2016

http://brianaspinall.com/tedx-talks/

MORE FROM CODEBREAKER!

CODE BREAKER:

15+ Ways To Get Started With Coding!

Increase Creativity, Remix Assessment And Develop A Class Of Coder Ninjas!

BLOCK BREAKER:

Building Knowledge And Amplifying Voice One Minecraft Block At A Time!

SCRATCHING THE SURFACE:

An Intro To Coding In Middle School

THINK LIKE A CODER!

Connecting Computational Thinking to Everyday Activities

Co-author:
Deanna Pecaski McLennan

HALLWAY CONNECTIONS:

Autism and Coding

By: Maggie Fay

GRACIE:

An Innovator Doesn't Complain About The Problem. She Solves It!

By: Daphne McMenemy

Made in the USA
Monee, IL
02 May 2020